W9-AEM-342

Building Global Mindsets

Building Global Mindsets

An Attention-Based Perspective

Cyril Bouquet

First published 2005 by
PALGRAVE MACMILLAN
Houndmills, Basingstoke, Hampshire RG21 6XS and
175 Fifth Avenue, New York, N. Y. 10010
Companies and representatives throughout the world

PALGRAVE MACMILLAN is the global academic imprint of the Palgrave Macmillan division of St. Martin's Press, LLC and of Palgrave Macmillan Ltd. Macmillan® is a registered trademark in the United States, United Kingdom and other countries. Palgrave is a registered trademark in the European Union and other countries.

ISBN-13: 978–1–4039–4648–5
ISBN-10: 1–4039–4648–5

This book is printed on paper suitable for recycling and made from fully managed and sustained forest sources.

A catalogue record for this book is available from the British Library.

Library of Congress Cataloging-in-Publication Data
Bouquet, Cyril.
    Building global mindsets : an attention-based perspective / Cyril Bouquet.
        p. cm.
    Includes bibliographical references and index.
    ISBN 1–4039–4648–5
        1. International business enterprises–Management. 2. Attention–Economic aspects. 3. Selectivity (Psychology) 4. Cosmopolitanism. 5. Corporate culture. I. Title: Global mindsets : an attention-based perspective. II. Title.

HD62.4.B68 2005
658.049–dc22   2004059164

10   9   8   7   6   5   4   3   2   1
14   13   12   11   10   09   08   07   06   05

Printed and bound in Great Britain by
Antony Rowe Ltd, Chippenham and Eastbourne

*This book is dedicated to
my grandmother*

Contents

List of Tables

List of Figures

Preface

I first discussed the concept of "attention" with Professor Allen Morrison at the Richard Ivey School of Business. It was one of our first meetings, Allen was just about to have breakfast, and I knew that his morning time was precious. "What do you want to do research on, Cyril?" Allen asked between bites of his chocolate muffin. "I'm really interested in why companies are struggling so hard to achieve the alleged benefits of globalization," I replied with a poorly disguised sense of trepidation and anxiety. After all, the issue I suggested was generic enough and unlikely to be at the top of Allen's current research preoccupations. "Why don't you look at attention?" Allen quickly replied. "Globalization constitutes a serious cognitive challenge for managers who have little attention to spare." Our active research collaboration began that January morning in 1999 and has continued since then.

At that time, it was frequently argued in international management literature that for a multinational enterprise (MNE) to be successful, it was not enough simply to sell products on a global basis, or to build up a network of value-adding activities around the world. Rather, the challenge for competitive success had become one of tapping into and leveraging underexploited pockets of knowledge and expertise dispersed throughout the world (Bartlett & Ghoshal, 1989; Doz, Santos, & Williamson, 2001). Inevitably, this imperative would place substantial pressures on MNEs and their top management teams to think and act in new and multi-faceted ways (Hamel & Prahalad, 1985). Among other things, careful attention was required to assess the relevance of events, trends, opportunities and threats that are often tacit and embedded in distant or unfamiliar environments (Gomes-Mejia & Palich, 1997).

I wrote this book convinced that the topic of attention offered an entirely new perspective on issues relating to global leadership and to the strategic management of MNEs. Allen and I interviewed a number of senior executives for this research. One of them thought a colleague was paying huge attention to the Japanese market as evidenced by his frequent trips to Japan. But our research revealed that while he was traveling to Japan every eight weeks, he watched US movies on the airplane trip, stayed at a US hotel chain in Tokyo, and had few interactions with local customers or suppliers. His typical day in Tokyo consisted of an 8:30am trip from the hotel to the company's local office, meetings with American expatriate managers, some office work which included frequent phone calls back to the US and work on home-office email, and then a return trip to the hotel at about 5:30pm. How much attention was he really paying to Japanese issues?

Insights gleaned from such conversations motivated me to write a PhD dissertation on the topic of attention. This three-year multiphased research project involved some of the most exciting experiences. I started the research by conducting eighteen in-depth field interviews in thirteen different MNEs. This phase allowed me to conduct a preliminary – largely inductive – observation of company practices that proved to be immensely useful for defining the research objectives and developing insights as well as hypotheses related to this study's areas of enquiry. The second stage of the research involved a cross-national survey of 136 MNEs with head-offices in six different countries (USA, Canada, France, Germany, United Kingdom, and Japan.) This quantitative phase was concerned with issues of reliability, validity, and hypothesis testing, using principal component analysis and multivariate regression analysis techniques. The third stage of the dissertation involved semi-structured post-test interviews with ten senior executives in nine different MNEs. The objective of these final conversations was to confirm my interpretation of the survey results by talking to those who have a direct and strategic stake in the issues at hand.

As things were progressing, it was obvious that I was "on to something." Many academics worldwide became interested in the ideas that Allen and I put forward, recognizing that it had become absolutely critical for MNEs to be at least as much concerned with the allocation of management attention as they are with the positioning of worldwide activities. Clearly, building global mindsets was still an important priority for companies, as important issues originating in foreign locations would typically receive relatively little attention at the corporate center (Green, Hassan, Immelt, Marks, & Meiland, 2003; Ohmae, 1989). For example, paralleling the "home-country investment bias" that is often discussed in the finance literature (Coval & Moskowitz, 1999), Canadian companies are twenty-two times more likely to trade with fellow compatriots than with companies equally distant but residing in the United States (McCallum, 1995). And in the US, under nine percent of patents come from research conducted abroad!

How can we explain the persistence of such parochial behaviors in the "global village" type of world that top executives inhabit? After all, previous studies have repeatedly argued that the more global the mindset, the better the performance (Calof & Beamish, 1994; Murtha, Lenway, & Bagozzi, 1998; Perlmutter, 1969). Through the research reported in this book, a more complicated, efficiency-based, story became apparent. Specifically, there may be limiting, or even diminishing returns to internationalizing the cognitions and actions of MNE executives. While companies experience lower performance levels when their top executives pay virtually no attention to foreign markets, the capacity to gain insight into what is happening in the farther corners of the business world must also be weighed against the opportunity cost of neglecting issues in the immediate task environment. Building global mindsets is not an objective that companies should pursue indefinitely. There is an optimal threshold to be found, as too much attention to international issues can also be drastically detrimental to the overall performance of a firm. It is best to think of the relationship between international attention and firm performance in curvilinear terms.

While I believe this book to be the first one specifically dedicated to the attention concept within the specific context of international activity, I also know that I am not the first person to think or write about attention in the management literature. The topic was first introduced to Allen by Tom Davenport and John Beck at the Accenture Institute for Strategic Change as they were starting to work on their new research project, a book called "The Attention Economy." In the academic sphere, William Ocasio built on the work of Herbert Simon and other theorists from the Carnegie School to present a promising "attention-based view of the firm," which may well represent a new field of management research. Hansen and Haas, from Harvard Business School, developed a model of electronic document dissemination in a management consulting company that effectively illustrated the dynamics of attention processing in competitive knowledge markets. I am grateful to these intellectual predecessors for their writings on attention, which served as a foundation for the ideas contained in this book.

There is a burgeoning list of people who have given me constructive criticism and contributed in some way to this book. First, my chief dissertation advisor, Professor Allen Morrison has been an invaluable resource and a great personal mentor. His patience, encouragement and support were essential as I was trying to find my way from an early stage conceptualization of the research to the final draft. His outstanding work ethic, coupled with true genuine intellectual curiosity, and relentless attention to the dual imperative of academic rigor and managerial relevance are qualities that I shall strive to emulate. I also owe great intellectual and personal support to Professor Julian Birkinshaw, at London Business School. Julian contributed insights that significantly improved the quality of my thinking. He also forced me to conceptualize the research in the context of issues that are central to the field of international management strategy. Moreover, the direction he provided in the summer of 2002 when I visited London Business School was most essential in bringing structure and balance to my emerging research ideas.

Other contributors to this study include Professor Paul Beamish, who repeatedly emphasized the necessity to talk to managers in the field; Professors Tony Frost, Amy Hillman (Arizona State University), John Hulland (University of Pittsburgh), and Rod White who taught me a great deal about what constitutes "good" management research; Professors Tima Bansal, Jean-Phillipe Bonardi, Mason Carpenter (University of Wisconsin at Madison), Andrew Delios (National University of Singapore) and Susanne Schneider (HEC Lausanne) who provided timely feedback and invaluable help at various stages of the research. I exchanged ideas about the attention field of research with Udo Zander and Christian Czernich at the Stockholm School of economics. Gerard Sanders (Brigham Young University) also contributed insights in the latter stages of the research. I also owe special thanks to Dean Larry Tapp for securing access to essential research sites, and to Jodi Guthrie for transcribing many of the field interviews.

On a more personal note, I would like to recognize my colleagues and mentors at the University of Ottawa, and more particularly George Hénault and Jean-Louis Schaan, for stimulating my interests for an academic career. I feel greatly indebted to them. I would like to thank my family and friends for the moral and emotional support they provided at all times. I couldn't have done it without the un-wavering love and support of my grandmother. And the numerous sacrifices of my parents made it possible for me to "just do it." Finally, I am grateful to my fellow doctoral student colleagues and friends, Maxime Charlebois, Anthony Goerzen, and Yany Gregoire who provided an essential support system in the fabulous town of London, ON. I am also personally most grateful to my girlfriend Melanie. She represents the future I wish to understand.

To all these people and others, I would like to express my sincere thanks.

Foreword

One of the most common refrains in companies that aspire to be global is the need for a global "mindset" – a way of looking at the world that transcends the parochial demands of individual countries. Some of the more celebrated multinational companies, including ABB, Nestle, and Nokia, have put their global mindset at the centre of the corporate identity. Other equally-successful companies, including GE, Toyota, and Daimler Benz, have seen the creation of a global mindset as an important facilitator of international development beyond their strong home-market position.

Global mindset is an alluring concept. The trouble with alluring concepts is they get overused, they get misapplied, and they easily lose their real meaning. This has happened to core competence, and to some degree with market orientation, competitive advantage, and corporate culture. And global mindset runs the risk of going the same way. For example, most people are familiar with the motto "think global, act local"; but cross-cultural expert Geert Hofstede has put forward a strong argument that it should be the reverse – "think local, act global". As he says, your national cultural roots make thinking "local" almost by definition; what matters for global companies is that this local thinking is translated into action that can be leveraged on a global basis.

Indeed, as you read the literature on global mindset, it becomes clear that there is little agreement on what exactly it means, on how it is developed, or even whether it is actually that important in the first place. Global mindset has been measured in terms of the cognitive maps of executives, the demographic backgrounds of top managers, and the practices and policies of the firm. Each approach has its own logic, but taken as a whole the picture is fragmented and confusing.

Cyril Bouquet's research is a breath of fresh air in this debate. He decided to take an entirely new angle on global mindset by studying what executives actually *do* – what they spend their time on, and what issues they give attention to. Purists may argue that

action and attention are not the same as mindset. Indeed they
are not. But they are certainly overlapping concepts, and they
provide a more direct and concrete way of getting to the heart of
the decision-making and action in the firm.

Moreover, by adopting the so-called attention based view of the
firm, Cyril was able to develop new insights into *how* a global
mindset is developed, and how valuable it is to the multinational
company. The results are clear-cut. If you want your executives to
devote their attention to international issues, don't assume that
they will automatically pick up the cues from the international
environment in which they are working; instead, you need to invest
in so-called *attention structures* that channel executive attention and
time towards those potentially salient issues. There is also a corporate performance implication: attention to international issues is a
good thing, but too much is bad. Intuitively this makes sense, but
Cyril's work is the first time this has been shown in a systematic
way.

I believe this is an important book: its findings are insightful, and
it is very well grounded in the academic literature. It shows the
power of combining a very practical research question in one area
with a body of theory from a different area. And it offers implications for both. I trust you will enjoy reading this work as much as
I did.

Professor Julian Birkinshaw
London Business School

1

A New Perspective on Global Mindsets

In March 1995, Michael Smith (fictitious name) paid $490,000 for a 1981 Beech Duke aircraft. A bargain, thought Smith, a retired fighter pilot with a long-time passion for aerial photography who had just retired from the Navy. In the summer of 1999, Smith scheduled one of his favorite flights over the Pacific Coast. As usual, he stuck two fingers into the tank to ensure fuel was at the top, before departing the local county airport. Winds were calm, and visibility was high. "The perfect conditions to shoot," thought Smith, while he and his wife were getting ready for an exciting photo session.

Forty minutes into the flight, Smith noticed the engine was emitting a lower pitch sound, not the high pitch sound he was used to hearing. He scanned his gauges, only to discover that his fuel had dropped to zero. In total disbelief, Smith looked at the wings, convinced he would see fuel pouring out of some sort of fuel tank rupture. But to his horror and dismay, there was no leakage. With no airport nearby, the engine came to a complete stop. Incredibly, Smith managed to land on a hard dirt road just besides a large cotton field.

What could have possibly gone wrong? In the report that he submitted to the Aviation Safety Reporting System (ASRS)[1] Smith indicated the following:

> It is obvious that I was complacent and inattentive, my thoughts on the photo work. My strong expectation was to find full tanks,

---

[1] ASRS is a NASA program that compiles data about near miss accidents to identify and prevent risk factors. The program's web site can be accessed at http://asrs.arc.nasa.gov/.

and somehow believed I felt gas at the top. That I didn't visually confirm it, and didn't check the fuel quantity indicators becomes more unbelievable every time I think about it.

Sometimes, accidents of this kind are the result of incompetence or experience deficit. But this forced landing was the first disturbing incident ever experienced by Smith in thirty one years of flying, much of it as a Navy pilot. Clearly, this accident was not related to poor training. It was a problem of *attention*. Smith had looked at the trip as just another routine flight, something he had done thousands of times in the past. He had stuck two fingers into the tank and felt safe, but this heuristic was so automatic that it was heavily susceptible to mindlessness on his part. Without ever realizing it, Smith had set himself mentally not to pay as much attention as he should to flying and navigating the aircraft. All of his thoughts were focused, instead, on the photo-job.

Unfortunately, there is no such thing as an ordinary trip. Flying an aircraft, like managing a global company, requires the full engagement of every pilot's mind. How many firms have crashed internationally because their top executives could not give global markets all the attention they deserved? In a world of perpetual "infoglut," paying attention to international business matters is often down the list of priorities for many managers. The results can potentially be catastrophic.

This chapter accomplishes several tasks that provide the foundation for the rest of this study. It starts by discussing the motivation of this research; namely, the impact that globalization exerts on MNEs and their top management teams. A new conceptualization of global mindset is then put forward. The proposed theoretical approach consists of going beyond the study of cognitive maps to investigate, instead, the day-to-day behaviors of MNE top executives. This approach makes it possible to find out whether and how managers at the top pay careful attention – as a group – to international issues in their decision-making activities. This attention focus is argued to constitute a critical manifestation of a global mindset that possesses important implications for MNEs. The remainder of this chapter presents the research methodology, key summary results, and a brief research outline.

1.1   What is this book about?

During the last twenty years, the increasing economic interdependence of nations has fundamentally altered the competitive landscape for most companies throughout the world. Some of the world's poorest countries (e.g. Brazil, China, India, Indonesia and Russia), each with GDPs larger than $100 billion and populations over 150 million, have embraced free-market ideology, liberalized investment regimes, and started to catch up with advanced economies in terms of competition, innovation, and faster economic growth (Garten, 1997). Rapid advances in communication technologies have also reduced the costs of negotiating, monitoring, and enforcing international business transactions. As a result, MNEs are assumed to operate in a "new global age" where securing a commanding global presence is a given that does not bear discussion. According to Govindarajan and Gupta (1998: 3), "virtually any company today that seeks to grow has little choice but to go where the growth is. For the vast majority of the world's top 500 industrial corporations, such growth is rarely in the home market."

Recent models of the MNE – which include the heterarchy (Hedlund, 1986), the multifocal organization (Prahalad & Doz, 1987), the transnational organization (Bartlett & Ghoshal, 1989), the horizontal organization (White & Poynter, 1990), and the meta-national organization (Doz et al., 2001) – all suggest that for a multinational enterprise (MNE) to be successful, it is not enough simply to sell products on a global basis, or to build up a network of value-adding activities around the world. Rather, the challenge for competitive success is to tap into and leverage underexploited pockets of knowledge and expertise that are dispersed throughout the world (Bartlett & Ghoshal, 1989; Doz, Santos, & Williamson, 2001). This places important pressures on MNEs and their top executives who must think and act in new and multi-faceted ways (Hamel & Prahalad, 1985), as illustrated in Table 1-1.

One of the key current challenges for MNEs, Doz et al. (2001) argue, is "to break-free of geography." In a related vein, Kanter (1995) suggests that cosmopolitan thinking – meaning, the ability to "tear down the invisible walls between countries, companies, cultures, customers, suppliers, and departments and levels within organizations, replacing walls that divide with bridges that link" –

Table 1-1   Skills and Capabilities that CEOs Believe They Need to Improve

	A Great Deal	Some	Not Much	None	Don't Know
Ability to think globally	72%	25%	2%	–	2%
Ability to execute strategies successfully	66%	28%	4%	–	2%
Flexibility in a changing world	63%	31%	4%	*	2%
Ability to develop appropriate strategies	60%	34%	4%	–	1%
Ability to rapidly redefine their business	54%	35%	8%	1%	2%
Understanding new technologies	52%	38%	8%	*	2%
Ability to work well with different stakeholders	50%	41%	7%	1%	1%
Ability to create a learning organization	49%	40%	8%	–	3%
Ability to make the right bets about the future	43%	40%	13%	1%	3%
Ability to be a visible, articulate, charismatic leader	41%	39%	17%	1%	2%

Source: The nation's CEOs look to the future, Foundation for the Malcom Baldridge National Quality Award, Study No. 818407, July 1998. Reprinted in Davenport and Beck (2001: 162.) * Indicates less than one percent.

has become an important part of the responsibilities of top management (1995: 327).

To respond to these needs, companies have taken serious initiatives such as increasing the international composition of their top teams and boards. Between 1995 and 1998, the proportion of companies worldwide with at least one foreign director has increased from 39 percent to 60 percent (Conference Board, 1999). Increasingly, CEOs themselves are being selected for their international competencies. Consider the case of Jacques Nasser who was appointed as President and CEO of Ford Motors Company when Trotman retired in 1998. While Nasser had worked for Ford for over 30 years, only 6 of those years were actually spent in Dearborn. Born in a mountain village in Lebanon and raised in Australia from the age of 4, Nasser has held key posts in Australia, Thailand, the Philippines, Venezuela, Mexico, Argentina, Brazil, and Europe. He has a degree in international business and speaks five languages.

Other members of Ford's top management group also have substantial international experience.

Nevertheless, many observers feel that not enough has been done to build global mindsets in MNEs (Green, Hassan, Immelt, Marks, & Meiland, 2003; Ohmae, 1989). Important issues originating in foreign locations are getting relatively little attention at the corporate center. For example, paralleling the "home-country investment bias" often discussed in the finance literature (Coval & Moskowitz, 1999), Canadian companies are twenty-two times more likely to trade with fellow compatriots than with companies equally distant but residing in the United States (McCallum, 1995). And in the US, under nine percent of patents come from research conducted abroad. Dunning (1996) concluded in his survey of the world's largest MNEs that they "perceived that their domestic operations and/or indigenous resources and capabilities of their home-countries continued to provide the main source of competitiveness – especially in terms of technological capacity and skilled professional manpower."

1.2 Global mindsets: what do we know?

Researchers have used the term "global mindset" to refer to the general ability to think on a global scale. A starting point for any discussion of global mindsets is Perlmutter's (1969) well-known distinction between ethnocentric (home-country mindset), polycentric (host-country mindset), and geocentric (global mindset) MNEs, but there has been a steady stream of research ever since. Perlmutter's work was picked up by Bartlett and Ghoshal (1989) who developed the global mindset concept further, though preferring the term "transnational mentality." During the 1990s, a series of studies approached the concept of global mindset in rather different ways (Calof & Beamish, 1994; Calori, Johnson, & Sarnin, 1994; Gupta & Govindarajan, 2002; Jeannet, 2000; Kobrin, 1994; Murtha et al., 1998). Table 1-2 provides a summary of the definitions, measures, and findings of these studies.

Definitions. At first, a close examination of this literature reveals diverse definitions of the global mindset concept. It has been defined in terms of a state-of-mind (Jeannet, 2000; Perlmutter, 1969), a predisposition (Fayerweather, 1969), an attitude (Calof & Beamish, 1994), or a mentality (Bartlett & Ghoshal, 1989; Prahalad & Doz, 1987) that predisposes managers to embrace cultural diversity. Calori et al. (1994) and Govindarajan and Gupta (2001) define global mindset in terms of a knowledge structure that guides and organizes managerial representations of the world. Sambharya (1996) takes a slightly different approach by examining the cognitive states, beliefs and values of top team members. A commonality across these definitions is that a global mindset allows individual executives, teams, and entire organizations to understand a business or market without regard to country boundaries (Kobrin, 1994; Murtha, Lenway and Bagozzi, 1998; Perlmutter, 1969). It can be seen as a cognitive orientation that combines "an openness to and awareness of diversity across cultures and markets with a propensity and ability to synthesize across this diversity" (Govindarajan & Gupta, 2001: 111).

Measures. Researchers have used at least five different ways of operationalizing the concept of global mindset. Calori et al. (1994) utilize cognitive mapping techniques established by Huff (1990) to tap into the complexity and comprehensiveness of a CEO's knowledge structure. Govindarajan and Gupta (2001) employ a series of diagnostic questions that examine various firm-level practices. Sambharya measures the international experience of a top team as a proxy for its international values and beliefs. Kobrin (1994) focuses on a firm's international human resource policies as the key indicator of geocentrism. And Murtha et al. (1998), Calof and Beamish (1994), and Jeannet (2000) measure a combination of individual attitudes, skills, and behaviors – such as traveling to foreign locations, or discussing international business issues in executive committee meetings.

Findings. A review of the research reveals that there is only limited agreement regarding the antecedents and consequences of global mindsets. In terms of antecedents, Bartlett and Ghoshal (1989) argue that a firm's administrative heritage is the key determinant of mindsets, Calori et al. (1994) focus on the complexity of the international environment, and Sambharya (1996) assumes that individual experience is critical. A number of researchers, including Gupta and Govindarajan (2002), Jeannet (2000), and Bartlett and Ghoshal (1989) have also emphasized the role of company practices in shaping the global mindsets of individual managers. These practices include training programs, international assignments, and job rotations across countries.

Table 1-2   Prior Research on Global Mindset

Study	Definition of Global Mindset	Operationalization of Global Mindset	Major Findings
Perlmutter (1969), Heenan and Perlmutter (1979)	Geocentrism is a global systems approach to decision making or state of mind where "HQ and subsidiaries see themselves as part of an organic worldwide entity...good ideas come from any country and go to any country within the firm" (1979: 21).	Global mindset is best measured by managerial attitudes. Other useful indices include the proportion of nationals in different countries holding equity and the number of foreign nationals who have reached top positions (1969: page 11).	Geocentrism is hypothesized to lead to "a more powerful total company, a better quality of products and services, worldwide utilization of best resources, improvement of local company management, and last but not least, more profit" (1969: 16).
Fayerweather (1969), Prahalad and Doz (1987), Bartlett and Ghoshal (1998)	A Transnational mentality is the capacity to deliver global integration, national responsiveness, and worldwide learning simultaneously ("a matrix in the minds of managers.")	A Transnational mentality is rooted in a firm's administrative heritage and evolves according to changes in firm structure, systems and culture.	A Transnational mentality is hypothesized to lead to superior long-run performance.
Calof and Beamish (1994)	Centricity is defined as a person's attitude towards foreign cultures. Geocentrism can be characterized by the following factors: "all major decisions are made centrally,... substantial	Respondents selected geocentrism, ethnocentrism, or polycentrism as their primary orientation (following descriptions of brief company profiles associated with each of these orientations.)	Of a sample of 38 Canadian firms, those that characterized themselves as geocentric had significantly greater international sales and export intensity than those that characterized themselves as ethnocentric or polycentric.

Table 1-2   Prior Research on Global Mindset – *continued*

Study	Definition of Global Mindset	Operationalization of Global Mindset	Major Findings
	coordination exists between offices ..., and focus is on global systems."		
Kobrin (1994)	Geocentrism defined using Heenan and Perlmutter (1979) above.	Five-item geocentrism index consists of questions relating to international human resource policies, e.g. "In the next decade I expect to see a non-US CEO in my firm."	Of a sample of 68 US manufacturing firms, a significant correlation is found between geocentrism and geographic scope (sales, employees overseas), but there is no relationship between geocentrism and global strategy.
Calori, Johnson and Sarnin (1994)	Global mindset is viewed as a cognitive structure or mental map that allows a CEO to comprehend the complexity of a firm's worldwide environment.	Cognitive complexity of a CEO is operationalized in terms of the number of constructs, and density of links between constructs, for his/her cognitive map.	Of a sample of 26 companies, a significant correlation exists between the geographic scope of a firm and the CEO's cognitive complexity.
Sambharya (1996)	Study taps into the "cognitive state" or "beliefs and values" of a top team.	Global mindset is measured by the international work experience of top team members.	Of a sample of 54 US manufacturing firms, a significant correlation is found between international experience at the top and international diversification.

Table 1-2 Prior Research on Global Mindset – *continued*

Study	Definition of Global Mindset	Operationalization of Global Mindset	Major Findings
Murtha, Lenway, Bagozzi (1998)	Global mindset defined using Fayerweather (1969), Prahalad and Doz (1981, 1987), and Bartlett and Ghoshal (1989).	Global mindset is measured using a multi-item questionnaire with sub-constructs relating to integration, responsiveness, coordination, career opportunities, global accountability, and meaning of globalization.	Of a sample of 370 individuals taken from a single MNE, mindsets are seen to evolve over a three-year period in line with an overall strategic change process.
Rhinesmith (1993), and Jeannet (2000)	Global mindset is a state of mind able to understand a business, an industry, or a particular market on a global basis.	Global mindset is described in a series of cross cultural skills (mastering foreign languages) and behaviors (e.g. traveling extensively around the world.)	Global mindset is hypothesized to lead to superior overall global performance.
Govindarajan and Gupta (2001)	Global mindset is defined (page 111) as a "knowledge structure ... that combines an openness to and awareness of diversity across cultures and markets with a propensity and ability to synthesize across this diversity."	Measured through a series of diagnostic questions pertaining to scanning, hiring, and learning behaviors. For example, is your company a leader (rather than a laggard) in your industry in discovering and pursuing emerging market opportunities in all corners of the world?	Global mindset is hypothesized to lead to superior overall global performance.

Figure 1-1 Antecedents and Implications of a Global Mindset

However, these researchers have neglected to either discuss how these mechanisms collectively interact to impact global mindsets, or to examine the relative effectiveness of the different approaches available to MNEs. If a company wants to effectively increase global mindsets, where should it start? More generally, can companies create a systemic infrastructure to ensure that mindsets are consistent with key strategic objectives? These are important questions to which the existing literature on global mindsets offers only limited answers.

In terms of consequences, many argue that global mindsets lead to more geocentric staffing decisions, such as drawing on a worldwide pool of human talent or local nationals (rather than company expatriates) to fill key positions in foreign subsidiaries (Perlmutter, 1969). Similarly, many suggest that global mindsets lead to superior firm performance, but this assumption lacks strong empirical support (Bartlett & Ghoshal, 1989; Govindarajan & Gupta, 2001; Jeannet, 2000; Kanter, 1994). Finally, several studies show that global mindsets are associated with greater international scope (Calof and Beamish, 1994; Kobrin, 1994; Sumbharya, 1996). However, none of these studies are able to indicate causality. Indeed, while a global mindset is commonly acknowledged to enhance the international scope of MNEs, the reverse logic can be equally compelling. Figure 1-1 integrates these different perspectives.

1.3   A new conceptualization of the phenomenon

This study advances a new conceptualization of global mindsets that integrates the different views found in the prior literature. Specifically, it draws on the theory of attention (Hansen & Haas, 2001; Ocasio, 1997) to develop the concept of international attention, which can be seen as a prime manifestation of a global mindset. The assumption behind this approach is that the behaviors that top managers demonstrate through decision-making indicate the degree to which the top team as a whole has a global mindset. This research provides a multi-level theory that articulates the linkages between the attention of individual managers, groups, and the entire organization.

While still recognizing the importance of knowledge structures, attitudes and skills in shaping decision-making, it is suggested that what really matters is how individuals behave in practice. Although there may be some advantages in arguing that the best measure of a global mindset is some sort of cognitive map, two problems are associated with this approach. First, cognitive mapping techniques are extremely laborious and have often resulted in inconclusive findings (Calori et al., 1994; Huff, 1990). As pointed out by Huff (1990), it is not easy to "read" the content of managers' minds in ways that are reliable and informative. Second, in those cases where a mismatch exists between what top managers believe is important and what they do, it is arguably more useful to focus on what they do, because that is what drives the subsequent behaviors of the MNEs.

Consequently, this research uses a behavioral approach to examine the global mindset phenomenon; meaning, it focuses on the actual (and more readily observable) time and effort that top team members devote to making sense of international issues, both for themselves and for the benefit of an MNE overall. This focus upon international issues includes attention given to events, developments, and trends that originate in distant locations where an MNE may or may not maintain operations on the ground, but where there might be potential implications for firm performance.

1.4 Expected contributions

By adopting a behavioral approach to the global mindset phenomenon, this study addresses one of the Achilles' heels of top management research; namely, the lack of studies that look – either through direct observation, field interviews or self-reported questionnaire data – at a company's top managers in action (Pettigrew, 1992). A gap often exists between the "espoused theories" of managers – what they think is important based on their cognitive orientations – and their "theories-in-use" – the behaviors they actually adopt in the course of decision-making (Argyris, 1976). For example, MNE top executives may espouse a global mindset by professing a view that globalization represents a critical challenge for the company and yet be reluctant to visit important customers abroad, and regularly fail to include salient international items to the agenda of executive committee meetings.

This study proposes to strengthen the role of behavior in the study of global mindsets by introducing the concept of international attention.

Another contribution of this research is that it provides a useful way of thinking about the mechanisms through which top management behaviors are shaped; specifically, it examines the *attention structures* that firms create to channel the limited attention of managers towards certain activities and away from others. This contribution has important implications for the international management literature because it highlights the different approaches (and their relative effectiveness) firms can use to develop global mindsets. While it may not be possible to indefinitely control the attention of MNE top executives, it can be influenced in a significant way.

A third contribution of this research is that it improves our understanding of the relationship that global mindsets have with company performance. Traditionally, research has focused on the products, skills and assets that underlie MNE success, i.e. the "ownership" advantages that Dunning (1988) describes in his eclectic theory of the MNE. This research extends this general framework by investigating whether it improves firm performance to develop top executives who can step outside their comfort zones and attend to increasingly diverse, globally integrated environments. Finding the *optimal* threshold of attention that MNE top executives should give to international strategic issues constitutes an important challenge for MNEs, and one that may significantly add to the competitiveness of a firm overall.

1.5   Road map for the reader

This chapter has presented a brief introduction and overview of the underlying research phenomena associated with the concept of a global mindset. The balance of the research naturally splits into six chapters.

Chapter 2 reviews attention theories in three key disciplines: psychology, economics, and organization theory. This literature review generates insights that are pertinent to the research objectives previously identified.

Chapter 3 describes the field interviews that were used to clarify the global mindset construct and to assist in the development of an integrative conceptual framework.

Chapter 4 discusses the methodology for testing the hypotheses formulated in Chapter 3 using a cross-national mail survey of 136 MNEs of various sizes and industries.

In Chapter 5, the statistical analyses and results are presented and the post-hoc interviews are discussed.

Chapter 6 provides an interpretation of the major findings of this research, and further addresses three broad themes uncovered through this investigation of global mindsets within MNEs: (1) the MNE as a matrix of inter-connected minds, (2) global mindset and the concept of geographic competency, and (3) the viability of a number of alternate globalization strategies for MNEs.

Chapter 7, the final chapter of this research, relates this study's results to the prior relevant literature in international strategic management research, while also providing a discussion of associated methodological limitations and directions for future research.

2
A Review of Attention Theories

> Everyone knows what attention is. It is the taking posses-
> sion by the mind, in clear and vivid form, of one out of
> what seems several simultaneously possible objects or
> trains of thought. Focalization and concentration of con-
> sciousness are of its essence. It implies withdrawal from
> some things in order to deal effectively with others, and is
> a condition which has a real opposite in the confused,
> dazed, and scatter-brained state which in French is called
> distraction.
>
> William James, *The Principles of Psychology*
> (1890: 403–404)

With trillions of internal company documents circulating in corporate offices everyday, it's easy to lose sight of priorities by concentrating on the wrong signals. As globalization rapidly expands the
amount of information that potentially affects a firm's activities and
performance, an increasing number of managers must confront the
essential question: how can they best manage their own attention
and that of other subordinates in the organization to ensure appropriate sensitivity and receptivity to what is happening in the farther
corners of the business world? This chapter begins peeling the onion
by answering a set of fundamental questions: *What is attention?*
What are the economics of attention? How can the organization more
effectively regulate the process of attention allocation? The implications
for MNEs and the development of global mindsets are discussed
along each of these themes.

2.1   What is attention?

Early cognitive psychologists, such as James (1890) and Titchener (1908), were among the first to observe that the study of individual attention was of crucial concern. James and Titchener defined attention as a condition of selective awareness that determines what is and what is not perceived or remembered by individuals. For example, Titchener (1908) built on the work of Wundt and Judd (1897) to portray attention as a type of cognitive frame (a mindset) by which sensations and visual images acquire greater "clearness." But the inadequacies of the introspective analysis of attention, the only method available at the time, prevented the establishment of attention as a valid scientific concept.

The psychological school of behaviorism (Pavlov, 1960; Sokolov, 1963; Watson, 1914) rejected attention and other cognitive phenomena such as perception, free will, volition, and consciousness, for they believed such concepts had no utility in their systems of stimuli-response relations. Attention became a convenient label to designate physiological responses to sensory stimuli. For example, Pavlov (1960) studied the behavioral signs of attention in dogs such as pricked-up ears, the turning of the head towards a stimulus, increased muscular tension, as well as other behavioral changes detectable with instruments.

During World Wars I and II, new types of attention problems were manifest, such as monitoring radar devices, tracking enemy aircraft, and maintaining the vigilance of soldiers. Gradual skepticism with the behaviorist paradigm provoked an upsurge of research on attention-related phenomena. A major challenge, at this time, was to determine how people and managers kept from being mentally overwhelmed by the massive amount of stimulation that surrounded them. Several experiments were conducted to determine how subjects chose what to perceive and attend to, and what to ignore. Later, rapid advances in computers and information technologies suggested interesting analogies between machines and the functioning of human brains (for a review see Lachman, Lachman, & Butterfield, 1979).

Towards the end of the 1960s, the concept of attention had become one of the bedrocks of the entire psychology discipline (Moray, 1969), and possesses important applications for organization settings. At the individual level, this interest in attention has been based on the recognition that not everything we are exposed to becomes part of our conscious perceptual experience. Our central nervous system, like other types of communication conduits, would rapidly fail if overloaded with millions of external stimuli for which we had to attend. Therefore, people always make decisions with respect to those signals that they feel to be worthy of their attention. Similarly, at the organizational level, organizations have been described as systems of distributed attention in which the distinct focus of time and effort by decision makers are derived from the particular structures and processes that the company puts in place (Ocasio, 1997). It is generally accepted – in both the cognitive psychology and managerial cognition literatures – that attention involves both selective and intensive aspects. These will now be discussed in turn.

The selective aspects of attention. Attention has been described as a kind of filtering system that separates high priority from low-priority information, as illustrated in Miller's classic paper *The Magical Number Seven* (1956) that demonstrated how only seven aspects of a situation, plus or minus two, are activated in any choice situation. In cognitive psychology, the first complete and perhaps best known model of selective attention was developed by Broadbent (1958). He assumed that biological limitations within the observer determine the filtering process that is called attention. Broadbent's model, presented in Figure 2-1, argues that environmental signals are processed through parallel sensory channels before being held in a temporary buffer, where their basic properties are analyzed for basic physical features such as size and color (Broadbent, 1958). These signals then transit through a selective

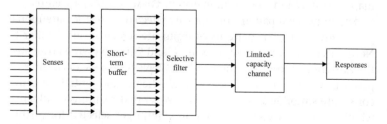

Figure 2-1   Broadbent's (1958) Bottleneck Model of Attention

filter that allows only those signals with the appropriate properties to proceed along the limited capacity channel for further analysis. Other signals are simply discarded.

Broadbent's (1958) model was later amended to allow for the possibility that the non-attended items are attenuated rather than completely blocked (Treisman, 1969). Deutsch and Deutsch (1963), Neisser (1976), and Norman (1969) subsequently proposed other models of selective attention that assumed that the filtering process would occur later, rather than sooner, in the sensory process. In these models, the mechanism of attention was examined alongside other mindset concepts that are equivalent to the notion of cognitive maps. For example, Neisser (1976) argued that "pre-attentive processes" activate and guide what people attend to and what they will process further. According to Norman (1969), the screening process is relatively "silent" in the sense that it always occurs outside conscious awareness, without the active control of individuals. People routinely watch their environments for things that require their attention, and in most situations this analysis occurs at the level of pattern recognition (Norman, 1969: 36).

> Attention mechanism cannot select intelligently among alternative channels of information unless it can first make a basic identification of the nature of the information. Suppose we hear several voices in the same hear. If we are to select one speaker, we must be able to extract from the complex acoustical waveform resulting from the combined voices, the features corresponding to each voice. This problem is one of pattern recognition.

Norman posited that people's abilities for pattern recognition are made possible by the use of mental schemes, which, like cognitive maps, are stored in long-term memory. These schemes are employed to determine what patterns of input are selected for further attentional processing, and what patterns of input are screened out. Similar to Norman's concept of schemes, Deutsch and Deutsch (1963) postulated the existence of "central structures" that have been developed through past learning experiences. These mental schemes and central structures constitute simplified theories of the world that seemingly influence whether and how certain incoming stimuli get selected for further attentional processing (White & Carlston, 1983).

In managerial cognition literature, the selective aspects of attention share a strong communality with the concepts of *problem recognition* (Cowan), *sensing* (Kiesler & Sproull, 1982), and *strategic issue diagnosis* (Dutton & Duncan, 1987; Dutton, Fahey, & Narayanan, 1983). At the individual level of analysis, managers have been described as "information workers" (McCall & Kaplan, 1985: 14) who must somehow sort the wheat from the chaff in the field of issues, events, opportunities, and threats facing them. Senior managers, in particular, rely on a limited stock of time and effort to oversee a vast array of activities (D'Aveni & MacMillan, 1990). Conversely, organizational attention refers to "the *distinct* focus of time and effort by the firm on a *particular* set of issues, problems, opportunities and threats" (Ocasio, 1997: 188, italics added).

The intensive aspects of attention. Kahneman (1973), Berlyne (1970), and others also argue that there is more to attention than mere selection of environmental stimuli. The degree or intensity with which attention is applied to a particular task or situation is also important. In this sense, attention corresponds to the deployment of "mental activity," "energy," and "cognitive resources" (Wickens, 1984). As Kahneman (1973: 3) comments: "any schoolboy knows that applying oneself is a matter of degree."

Similarly, in the social cognition literature, attention is presented as involving "active thinking" (Louis & Sutton, 1991), "mindfulness" (Laberge, 1995), and/or "heedful action" (Weick, 1993). As a result, several authors emphasize the fact that attention relates to how decision-makers focus their time and effort (D'Aveni & MacMillan, 1990; Hansen & Haas, 2001; Ocasio, 1997; Sproull, 1984). Conceptually, as illustrated in Figure 2-2, one may thus employ a continuum to characterize the kind of attention people will invest in a given task (Norman, 1969; Reger & Palmer, 1996; Shiffrin, 1988).

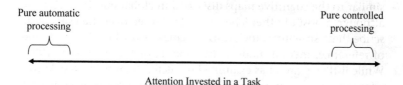

Figure 2-2   Attention as a Continuum of Higher Order Mental Activity

At one end of the continuum, a given task is conducted in a relatively effortless and unintentional manner, outside of people's conscious awareness (Kahneman & Treisman, 1984; Laberge & Samuels, 1974). This mode is highly dependent upon practice and habit, and might include such routine activities as combing one's hair or looking out a car window at familiar scenery. At the other hand of the continuum, the performance of a task involves effortful and deliberate cognitive processing (Langer, 1989; Logan, 1980; Uleman, 1989). Examples of this behavior would include performing complex problem solving in mathematics or public speaking. Like breathing, the terms "automatic" and "controlled" have often been used to describe attentional activities that approximate these respective poles (Shiffrin & Schneider, 1977). Interestingly, the same activity may require more or less attention depending on the skills of the person involved. A common example given to distinguish between controlled and automatic processing is learning to play a musical instrument like the piano. A novice player utilizes controlled processing to grasp the fundamentals of music theory, to learn the basics of the keyboard, and to progressively develop the listening skills of a promising musician. An experienced player utilizes automatic processing to achieve skillful performance without consciously thinking about it.

Implications for MNEs. In spite of the diversity of views presented on attention, on one point there is widespread agreement: attention is a selective process that focuses the mental energy of individual actors, and through them, entire organizations. As a result, one essential pre-requisite for determining whether a company's top executives will allocate attention towards international issues is the existence of knowledge structures that promote "an openness to and awareness of diversity across cultures and markets with a propensity and ability to synthesize across this diversity" (Govindarajan & Gupta, 2001: 111). These knowledge structures are similar to the cognitive maps discussed in global mindset literature, although a host of other labels have been used over the years to describe these structures, including schemas, heuristics, scripts, frames of reference, mental models, and dominant logics (Walsh, 1995). While little research has examined the determinants of these knowledge structures, generally international experience is recognized as being a key component (Black, Gregersen, Mendenhall, & Stroh,

1999a; Daily, Certo, & Dalton, 2000; Reuber & Fisher, 1997). In the next section, the work of micro-economists is reviewed to further our understanding of why top team managers invest attention the way they do in MNEs.

2.2   Economics of attention

The economics of attention are essentially concerned with the way in which the attention of a company's executives becomes allocated. A starting point for examining this issue is related to the concept of a market for attention, where information is plentiful and attention is scarce (Davenport & Beck, 2001; Hansen & Haas, 2001). As Simon (1982: 173–176) notes, "any fool with money" can obtain information on customers, technology, or competitors worldwide. But this wealth of information leads to a dearth of attention to individual data points. Hence, according to Simon, "a wealth of information creates a poverty of attention." While a market for attention exists throughout the entire organization, the ideas justifying its existence are particularly relevant in the higher levels of a firm's hierarchy. In particular, Simon (1997: 240) indicates:

> The bottleneck of attention becomes narrower and narrower as we move closer to the tops of organizations, where parallel processing capacity becomes less easy to provide without damaging the coordinating function that is a prime responsibility of these levels. Only a few items can simultaneously be on the active agenda at the top.

Top managers have been found to rely on a number of distinct strategies to avoid information overload. A key strategy used by managers consists of ignoring peripheral aspects of the entire situation in order to deal effectively with others. For example, March and Simon (1958: 11) present "a picture of a choosing, decision-making, problem-solving organism that can do only one or a few things at a time and that can attend to only a small part of the information recorded in its memory and presented by the environment." However, important opportunity costs may follow, since paying attention to some aspects of a total situation also means foregoing evaluation of other, perhaps more important, concerns.

Pricing Mechanisms Affecting the Competition for Attention. The economics of attention suggest that the attention allocation process is not random. Perhaps the strongest economically rational criteria available to a company's top executives in deciding how to allocate their limited time and effort among competing issues is to select those stimuli that are substantively the *best* in terms of a given utility function (Winter, 1987: 165). Of course, this maximizing approach to the problem of attention allocation presupposes the existence of economic agents who have considerable knowledge about the true economic value of incoming stimuli, and who are also perfect mathematicians with full computational abilities (Marschak & Radner, 1972). While elegant, this approach does not seem to correspond very well to the world of "real" managers who often use experience, judgment, and less-than-perfect agenda-setting techniques to navigate an enormous amount of potentially relevant information. Therefore, much like psychologists, economists recognize the importance of heuristics in helping company executives to prioritize among competing issues. For example, Radner (1975) proposes a model that describes the allocation of a manager's efforts among several competing projects for the purpose of cost reduction. In this model, the criterion for allocating attention to a project is determined by the content of the manager's cognitive maps, which includes heuristics such as the conservative thermostat cycle of "putting-out fires." This heuristic prescribes that *"Project A"* will receive attention if its costs rise by some predetermined fraction. However, as soon as the cost of *"Project A"* falls to the previous level, its urgency decreases, and attention is withdrawn.

Implications for MNEs. The economics of attention suggest that in many MNEs, the attention of top executives is likely to be focused on a few lead markets where the company exerts most of its strategic activity or on those markets with the biggest problems (Doz et al., 2001). Scanning remote parts of the world where the company is not well established would indeed represent an inefficient alternative in the minds of top executives, in that it would drain away scarce attentional resources. While often efficient, this selective focus of attention can also be problematic. Indeed, research demonstrates that important opportunities and threats often emerge in locations that may currently be peripheral parts of the world.

Neglecting these developments may create blind spots, where a company "will either not see the significance of events at all, will perceive them incorrectly, or will perceive them very slowly" (Porter, 1980: 59).

The next section builds on organization theory to discuss the mechanisms through which MNEs can intervene in the market for attention. In doing so, it also highlights the different approaches that MNEs can use to shape the international attention of top team members.

2.3 The regulation of attention in organizations

Ocasio (1997) proposed an innovative model of attentional processing in which the behavior of a firm is explained by how managers focus attention in their decision-making activities – and not simply by environmental influences. This attention-based framework describes a multi-level process spanning individual, social cognitive, and organizational levels of analysis. At the level of individual cognition, Ocasio argues that managers are selective in terms of the issues that enter consciousness at any given time (principle of selective attention). At the level of social cognition, and consistent with perspectives of social psychology, the characteristics of the contexts and situations to which decision-makers are exposed are described to determine how managers spend their time and effort as a group (principle of situated attention). At the organizational level, Ocasio emphasizes the role of attention structures in regulating the attention of individuals and groups throughout the multiple functions that take place within the organization (structural distribution of attention). The role of attention structures is discussed further below.

The role of attention structures. Organizational theorists introduced the term "attention structures" to describe the broad set of mechanisms and social rules by which companies channel and prioritize the attention of managers throughout the organization (March & Olsen, 1976; Ocasio, 1997). For example, March (1994) explains how deadlines, strategic initiatives, well-defined options, and evidence of failure contribute to more effectively structuring attention processing. In addition, Ocasio (1997), Davenport and Beck (2001), and Hoffman and Ocasio (2001) argue that attention is greatly affected by various elements of a company's organizational context, such as the set of assumptions, norms, values, and incentives that guide managers in their decision-making activities.

Attention structures comprise various controls, rewards, and punishments systems that are implemented throughout an organization (Burgelman, 1983a). At a more symbolic level, attention structures also include the particular beliefs, norms, and values that define what is central, enduring, and unique about the way a firm conducts business. For example, in their interpretation of Barnard's work, Levitt and March (1995: 13) equate the problem of organizing to "the construction of a moral order in which individual participants act in the name of the institution – not because it is in their self-interest to do so, but because they identify with the institution and are prepared to sacrifice some aspects of themselves for it."

Through their choices of attention structures, organizations act as "focusing devices that guide and channel the attention of decision-makers towards the achievement of overall organizational goals and purposes" (Czernich & Zander, 2000: 5). Significantly, the ordering of attentional preferences may not always be in tune with a firm's strategic priorities. Sometimes, the attention structures that channel attention towards certain activities and away from others may reflect past strategic objectives, and, thus, are no longer beneficial to a firm's performance. In other cases, the attention regulators may reflect the personal interests, values, and orientations of the most powerful organizational actors, and may therefore conflict with the organization's true purpose (Selznick, 1957).

Implications for MNEs. The literature reviewed in this section argues that the allocation of time and effort by a top team is best explained by the attention structures that an MNE puts in place. In other words, the amount of attention that top managers pay towards international issues owes very little to their prior experience/cognitive maps or to simple economic notions based on an MNE's administrative heritage. Rather, the specific structures, procedures, and processes that a firm puts in place to channel attention towards certain issues, activities, and tasks and away from others are seen as prime determinants of international attention. In this theoretical framework, some of the previously used measures of global mindset (e.g. international human resource policies, Kobrin, 1994; MNE rules and procedures, Murtha et al., 1998) are best understood as attention structures that influence the subsequent behaviors of top managers, rather than as measures of global mindset per se.

2.4 Summary

Attention does not consist of a unitary phenomenon. Rather, it involves a set of related cognitive phenomena that together indicate how individuals, and through them, top management teams and entire organizations, allocate their time, energy and effort among competing uses. Based on both logic and factual research data, it is likely that a principle of efficiency will typically lead managers to focus attention on a few "lead" markets where company is already well established to the detriment of more distant areas of the world, where critical developments may still happen. The inevitability of this logic suggests that MNEs face a relatively simple choice: they can design structures that promote a clear global perspective among managers, or accept the risk of letting blind spots in the company's radar screen. The next chapter develops a theory that further articulates the mechanics associated with this basic argument, while also shedding light on important performance implications.

3
Grounded Theory Development

Managers likely differ in their attention to the world. And through them, so do entire organizations. But until recently, assessing the implications of such differences has been a rather awkward enterprise dependent on the use of approximate time recording techniques, best recall, and direct observation procedures. This chapter uses methods that are largely inductive, qualitative, and non-statistical in nature, as well as insights from relevant international strategic management literature, to present ideas and research propositions that help companies (1) better diagnose the attention top executives give to international business matters; (2) identify a set of internationally-oriented tools through which they can more effectively direct the focusing of time and effort by managers; and (3) understand whether global thinking abilities can improve performance, or whether in fact a more parochial approach works just as well.

3.1 Qualitative interviews

Glaser and Strauss describe the principles of a grounded theory approach in their well-known observation of dying patients in medical institutions. Written as a polemic against *a priori*-theorizing, their original monograph was intended to encourage researchers to inductively generate theory from data that is systematically obtained and analyzed (Glaser & Strauss, 1967). In a grounded theory approach, the theorizing process moves from empirical observations to the development of concepts and their proposed relations. However, this process does not mean that researchers embark on a particular study without the general guidance of an orienting theoretical perspective. Rather, Glaser and Strauss emphasize the importance of making constant comparisons between the emerging theoretical framework and existing relevant disciplinary theory. A similar interplay between theory and empirical observation is used in the remaining of this chapter. The field research presented in this chapter involved in-depth face-to-face interviews with 18 senior executives. Because the purpose of this qualitative study was theory construction, special care was taken to ensure that the sample included top team members in a variety of functions (e.g. CEO, CFO, VP Leadership Development, VP Worldwide Sales, etc.) and industry sectors. Care was also taken to select large and heavily diversified MNEs (e.g. Bombardier), as well as small and more domestically focused companies (e.g. Campbell Aviation). Table 3-1 provides details on the interview sample.

Table 3-1   Exploratory Study Companies and Interviews

	Head-Office	$USm Sales	Respondents
1. Accelio	Ontario (CA)	114	1. VP and Chief Strategy Officer
2. Alcan	Quebec (CA)	9,148	2. Director Corporate Development
3. Bombardier	Quebec (CA)	10,705	3. Chairman Transportation 4. VP Leadership and Organization Development
4. Campbell Aviations	Virginia (USA)	NA	5. Co-founder and President
5. CCL Industries	Ontario (CA)	1,569	6. Chairman and CEO 7. SVP, and Chief Financial Officer 8. President CCL Label
6. Cognos	Ontario (CA)	386	9. VP, Product Services

Table 3-1 **Exploratory Study Companies and Interviews** – *continued*

	Head-Office	$USm Sales	Respondents
7. **Corel Corporation**	Ontario (CA)	283	10. EVP, Worldwide Sales
8. **Cuisine Solutions**	Virginia (USA)	28	11. VP, and Chief Financial Officer
9. **EssoAir International**	London (UK)	5.9	12. Director of Business Development
10. **Husky Injection Molding Systems**	Ontario (CA)	913	13. VP, Human Resources 14. VP, Marketing
11. **ICI**	London (UK)	9,356	15. VP, Organization Development
12. **Invensys**	London (UK)	9,939	16. Director Human Resource
13. **Maple Leaf Food**	Ontario (CA)	3,551	17. VP, Strategic Planning 18. VP Leadership Development

A total of thirteen companies were included in the sample. The companies were headquartered in Canada, the US, and the United Kingdom, and many individuals were interviewed in several organizations. The sample reflected a diverse set of positions and organizational contexts, and thus, it was deemed well suited to the generation of insights that might confirm, and possibly extend, insights gleaned from the literature review. Most companies were initially contacted via a personal letter and telephone follow-up. However, some companies were approached on a convenience basis, using personal or faculty contacts, the Dean's contacts, and/or the network of alumni from the Ivey Business School. Interviews were conducted incrementally to the point of theoretical saturation; meaning, they were conducted in a manner whereby further interviews resulted in little additional learning (Parkhe, 1993; Yin, 1989).

A list of questions was generated from the conclusions discussed in Chapter 2 (Table 3-2). With so many issues competing for

Table 3-2   Interview Questions

Confirming the Practical Relevance of the Research Phenomenon

---

1. What are the three things that keep you awake at night?
2. When you think of globalization, what do you think of?
3. Is your company's global presence a source of competitive advantage?
4. How difficult is it to become a successful global company?
5. What does it take to achieve global effectiveness?
6. Is it critical to have globally-oriented managers, and why?

Explicating What it Means to Have International Attention

---

7. When you think of international attention, what do you think of?
8. Who needs international attention in the organization?
9. How do you know whether a company's managers have international attention?

Research Objective 3: Developing Hypotheses

---

10. How can organizations foster international attention in top managers?

---

top management attention, it was deemed important to verify the practical relevance of the research phenomena by determining whether issues of globalization per se (including the globalization of managers within MNEs) are viewed as important items on the strategic agenda of the executives who were interviewed. Next, questions were used to clarify the key construct domain and to discover behaviors that represent good indicators of international attention. Finally, a question was asked in order to identify the structures and systems that MNEs use to influence how top team members invest attention in their decision-making activities. The initial questions were used to facilitate the emergence of a dialogue, or conversation, between the respondent and the interviewer. While these questions provided a general guide to structure each interview, not all questions could be asked to all respondents because of time constraints. In some cases, additional questions were used to follow-up on specific, largely idiosyncratic issues raised by the respondents during the course of the interviews. As well, it was often necessary to explain and clarify the questions in order to solicit stories and examples.

Personal interviews lasted approximately one hour. All conversations were audio taped and transcribed. Each respondent was subsequently asked to review, edit and release the complete interview record. This procedure gave the interviewees the opportunity to reflect upon what they had said, and to make any changes that they felt was necessary.

Data Analysis. The data was then analyzed using a standard three-step procedure (Butterfield, Trevino, & Ball, 1996; Glaser & Strauss, 1967). First, the answers to the different questions were broken down into recording units, which represent relevant and coherent fragments of text with a single meaning structure. According to Locke (2001), this fracturing of the data allows researchers to step back from the data, examine it microscopically (i.e. on a line-by-line basis), and conceptualize it in a new way that transcends the particular interview in which the data is embedded. Judgment was used to determine what constituted a recording unit. In some instances, a coherent fragment was made of a few words. In other instances, sentences or entire paragraphs could constitute a recording unit. Second, the recording units that were identified were compared and contrasted across respondents. Recording units that had similar or shared meanings were organized into emergent concept categories or themes, using the relevant literature as a guide to the classification process.

Verifying the practical relevance of the research phenomenon

To what extent do issues related to the human challenge of globalization preoccupy the top executives of MNEs today? The data reported below seeks to examine this overarching question.

"What are the three things that keep you awake at night?" The data pertaining to this question yielded 65 recording units that were organized in 10 salient conceptual categories, using the labels provided by Hoffman and Gopinath (1994) and Lyles (1990) as a guide to the classification process.

Table 3-3 shows the names and frequencies of the conceptual categories, as well as supporting examples of matching recording units. Collectively, this table represents a list of issues that are assumed to form part of the strategic agenda of a firm's top executives. This table shows that issues related to the research phenomenon are indeed important items on the agenda of MNE top executives. To begin, the majority of participants identified globalization matters (e.g. global strategy, the threat of competitors emerging from new locations, etc.)

Table 3-3   Things that Keep MNE Top Executives "Awake at Night"

Conceptual Categories	Freq.	Examples of Matching Recording Units
Globalization matters	14	*International competition from a pricing standpoint. We are a North American and European based manufacturer. We have competitors in other parts of the world that have a lower manufacturing cost base. How do you win at being a global manufacturer of a similar product is one of the things that keeps me awake at night.*
Industry dynamics, e.g. consolidation, new competitive threats, etc.	12	*The consolidation of the food industry. On our customer side, grocery retail stores are becoming larger and more powerful. On the processor side, we are seeing increasing investment by large US players in our domestic market. You are seeing a kind of harmonization of the North American marketplace, which changes the game for us.*
Domestic economy/general business climate, growth	9	*The economy and what is going on out there since September 11th and the long-term effects it may have on our business, our cash flows, and what we need to do with the rest of the company in a "down" market.*
Technology (e.g. Internet), innovation, and information	9	*The speed at which we develop new products and the necessity to always increase that speed and get more products to the market place that fit what the market needs.*
Competition for human talent, engaging people in a company's vision and values	8	*Wondering how are we going to attract, develop and retain talented people. We need more people that have a broad understanding of the business, of their functions, and of the purpose of the company. We are talking about people that have a view they are ready to share about what is important for the company. People that see themselves as being part of the organization, not only working for it.*
Reducing costs, improving efficiency, shareholder value	4	*The push on the cost side is an ongoing concern. What keeps me awake is trying to keep our focus on cost reduction.*
Organization change, business transformation, and increasing strategic flexibility	4	*Monitoring the pace of change and business transformation. With the rate of change in our market, it is very difficult to be on top of everything. We have just gone through a merger, and haven't come yet to a common understanding as to how the company is to operate.*

Table 3-3 Things that Keep MNE Top Executives "Awake at Night" – *continued*

Conceptual Categories	Freq.	Examples of Matching Recording Units
Customer loyalty/relationships	2	*Finally, it will be more and more difficult to differentiate our products, and we will have to do it through the people we employ, and the ability to have outstanding relationships and services with our customers.*
Other	2	*At any given time, a certain project on my list could keep me awake. It could be one thing today, and something wholly unrelated tomorrow: Things change so fast.*
	64	

as primary concerns for their company. Other executives noted that societal trends such as industry consolidation and the Internet are intensifying globalization pressures, with competition for human talent being the most immediate result.

For example, Tom Jakubowski, the Corporate Vice President of Strategic Planning at Maple Leaf Food, notes:

> The trends that we are seeing in international business – of consolidation and increasing globalization of the food industry – will impact us within Canada at Maple Leaf. The speed at which that happens may force us to potentially look to new global marketplaces, possibly even before we would have normally done it. We have to prepare as best as we can for globalization, but there are important difficulties such as not having the resources in place. These include financial resources, i.e. the capital to either grow organically or to make acquisitions. Even more critical are the management resources. Many companies tend to be relatively thin in terms of management talent that has the experience to compete effectively on the global stage.

"What do you think of when you think of globalization?" Depending on the unit of analysis (Table 3-4), several meanings of globalization were identified. At the macro level, globalization was often approached in terms of societal and industry dynamics. However, the majority of the interviewees adopted a company view of globalization. And interestingly, some respondents spontaneously tackled the cognitive side of globalization by mentioning company initiatives aimed at fostering the development of globally-oriented managers. In most cases, these views reflected concerns related to the ethnocentric tendencies of managers which appear to be still prevalent in many MNEs (Ohmae, 1989; Perlmutter, 1969). For example, and in line with Doz et al.'s (2001: 51) observation that the "primacy of the home-base" still exerts a strong impact on decision-making even in large geographically dispersed organizations, Geoff Tudhope, Vice President of Organization Development at ICI, observes:

> Globalization at ICI has traditionally meant the UK and Commonwealth countries. Trying to break out of this is very tough.

Ethnocentrism is an issue where we have mass. If you are big in one country, it creates a center of gravity problem. You don't realize it but you swamp everyone else.

"Is international attention key to globalization success?" This question was tackled in an indirect manner, through the use of Questions 3 to 6 in Table 3-2. Specifically, these questions run as follows: "Does your company's global presence provide a source of competitive advantage? How difficult is it to become a successful global company? What does it take to achieve global effectiveness? Is it critical to have globally-oriented managers, and why?" Respondents generally concluded that securing a commanding global presence was absolutely necessary to a company's survival. For example, Robert Hedley, Vice President Leadership Development at Maple Leaf Food, observes: "There is no doubt we cannot stay in Canada, or even just within North America. That is not an option." When asked what would happen if the company limited the scope of its global efforts, Hedley answered: "We would likely be bought out." Other benefits associated with becoming more international were also noted, as explained in the following passages.

- Guy Dupuis, Vice President Product Services of Cognos

  A lot of our customers are big customers and they are also thinking global. They want our software to run globally. They want services in different parts of the world. You must have global presence to operate successfully in the software industry.

- Donald Lang, President and CEO of CCL Industries

  Being more "international" allows us to get access to other technologies or best practices that you may not have locally. It also allows us to align ourselves with our customers, who like to conduct business with people who operate in more than one economy.

Nevertheless, several obstacles to a company's globalization efforts were also noted. For example, some respondents evoked the difficulty of managing across distance and multiple time zones. Others

Table 3-4 What Do You Think of When You Think of Globalization?

Unit of Analysis	Conceptual Categories	Examples of Matching Recording Units
Macro (7)	Openness of the world (3)	*I think of the removal of the borders. You cannot isolate yourself from country to country.*
	Industry dynamics (4)	*Globalization in the software industry is a fact. There are no barriers of entry to other countries any more. There are very few restrictions in terms of specialized technologies, such as encryption or decryption. When I look at our competition, we are competing with American companies, Swedish companies, German companies, French companies, Japanese companies, and the same applies to partnering. The software industry and globalization go hand in hand. It is almost impossible for any serious player not to be global.*
Company (14)	Developing global leaders, including global mindset (5)	*When I think of globalization, I think of how we can develop global mindsets by putting people in global environments. And that may consist of moving from Montreal to Berlin, Berlin to London UK, and London UK to somewhere else. We move a lot our top managers from place to place. We are constantly exposing our managers to international issues.*
	Strategic posture (3)	*I see two dimensions. One is getting revenues from a number of different geographic regions. But that is not the full picture. To me, a fully globalized company is one that doesn't just do business but that actually has assets in a number of different geographies.*
	Structures and processes (3)	*I think of it in terms of standardization. We think about processes when we think about globalization. It is about having the right processes around the world.*
	Decision-making (2)	*In our company we think about how we are going to refine our business model, and take that business model to other places in the world.*

Table 3-4 What Do You Think of When You Think of Globalization? – *continued*

Unit of Analysis	Conceptual Categories	Examples of Matching Recording Units
	Integrative views (1)	*So we are thinking about "where do we go?" Is it South America? Is it the United States? Is it Asia? Where do we go first? There is no doubt we cannot stay in Canada, or even just within North America. That is not an option.* *Globalization is about doing business in every country. It is everything: functions, processes, people. To be effective at globalization, you have to be able to tie it all together. Managers from both the US and UK are bad at thinking they are not the center of the world. Ninety-eight percent of the managers have no clue how to be global. Even if they are responsible for worldwide operations, they think of globalization concepts in terms of physical assets. If anything, they think "we are going to teach the rest of the world our way of doing things." There is a parallel between imperialism and people's conceptualization of globalization.*

cited a shortage of time to listen to and to understand foreign markets. Overall, many noted that achieving the advantages of globalization represented a complicated process that takes substantial time, patience, good strategic planning, and the right mix of organizational capabilities.

As Chris Trojanowski, Chief Strategy Officer of Accelio, observes:

> Companies have to understand the ripple effects throughout the organization that will result from making the decision to globalize. Expanding from North America to Europe requires knowledge of multiple languages, and it creates legal and currency challenges. Going to Japan is yet another challenge that requires a great deal of patience and relationship building. Globalization has to be a rational process of decision-making, justified by the size of the market, and the capabilities of the organization.

Jean-Yves Leblanc, Chairman of Bombardier Transportation, discusses in the following passage the set of organizational capabilities that may be required for global success:

> First of all, I would say the architecture of the organization, i.e. how it organizes. And that goes well beyond a simple organization structure. The proper architecture will help you empower your managers. How you design your architecture will determine whether you have a global perspective on things, whether you do draw upon global resources and whether your people can do well what you want them to do. The whole thing starts with the proper architecture.
>
> The second key issue is proper governance. We have been told a lot of things about governance, but there is a big difference between having a good, reliable and empowering governance, weak governance and no governance at all. You can easily see the difference when you benchmark companies. Proper governance gives you proper control over what's happening. And then, obviously enough, you need the best people. You also need to communicate very clearly your expectations to your people and keep a two-way channel of communication.

The data gathered from the other interviewees' responses was organized in ways that are consistent with Leblanc's view (Table 3-5).

Responses pertaining to issues of governance emphasized the need for globally oriented people. While some respondents foreground the necessity to increase cultural diversity within a top team and board, others explicitly mentioned the concept of global mindset. For example, Michel Jacques, Director of Corporate Development of Alcan, notes:

> You need to have people who have a global mindset. People who have experience and information expertise in various foreign markets. People who can appreciate the differences in working conditions, business habits, and business cultures. People who are aware of the different environments, whether legal, physical, or industrial. People who are familiar with the government relations throughout various countries.

Responses of this type were particularly important in justifying the practical relevance of the research phenomenon. The respondents also had much to say when asked to comment on the relative value of globalizing managerial attention. Among other things, the rapid internationalization of a company's major stakeholders (e.g. its customers and competitors) was often cited as a key element behind their company's motivation to foster global perspectives in managers. Chris Trojanowski, Chief Strategy Officer of Acceli, reports:

> Global mindsets are key, especially in markets like ours, which are in a constant state of flux and re-adjustment. Companies never know if there is a new competitor emerging in some part of the world. Also, there are many smart people around the world trying to figure out what the latest technology is, and the best ways to use it as a competitive advantage. We have to keep up or get behind. Right now, the entire world is the competitive arena.

Summary. This quote, like many others, reflects the perception that companies are operating in a new competitive landscape, where sources of knowledge and market intelligence are increasingly dispersed around the world. According to Doz et al. (2001), it has become difficult, if not impossible, for companies to designate the "lead markets" for most products and services, because promising technological breakthroughs are being developed in distant, sometimes

Table 3-5 What Does it Take to Achieve Global Effectiveness?

Themes	Conceptual Categories (Freq.)	Examples of Matching Categories
Architectural Design (10)	• Control and integration mechanisms (6)	You need to put in place global integration mechanisms. It helps the company bridge various global businesses operating in the same continent, say global packaging and global rolling.
	• Supporting logistics (1)	If we have global customers, they have to be supported twenty-four hours a day. At Accelio, we have three main support centers. One in Ottawa, one in Dublin and one in Tokyo. Our system is designed so that if a service call is placed from, for example, Dublin, the system can flow with the clock. Setting up a system like this is a tremendous challenge.
People and Governance (11)	• Developing globally-oriented managers (5)	The most important factor would be getting it right on the people side. If you have ten thousand employees, and half your sales are outside of North America, you should expect to see the management reflect that, and the Board of Directors too. If you go to say IBM, a company that probably does more than 50% of its sales outside the US, and you take a look at the construction of their Board and their top management team, you can see French, German, Chinese and Japanese people. You need to have a diversity of leadership to be successful in multiple continents and multiple countries.
	• Finding the right balance between local staff and expatriates (4)	It comes down to people. A KPMG survey done a number of years ago in the UK found that 70% of all North American companies that had businesses in the UK were managed by local management. From our experience, we had a lot of expatriates working over there and it was very difficult. When you go "global", I think you are better off putting in local management. However, doing this takes a lot of work to find the right people.

Table 3-5 What Does it Take to Achieve Global Effectiveness? – *continued*

Themes	Conceptual Categories (Freq.)	Examples of Matching Categories
Defining and communicating strategy (9)	• Communicating the company's strategy (4)	*The key thing is to make sure that the future of your company is well understood by the employees. Not the future in terms of the vision, but the way forward. This is fundamental, more than ever. If there is not a clear sense of direction, people will start going all sorts of avenues. They will pursue every opportunity. That will be a waste of time and energy. They will be collecting information and processing all sort of things that are not vital to where the company wants to go.*
	• Business model (3)	*We have a business model that has come along, and that works well here in Canada. You need to be able to develop competencies that you can go global with and our implementation of vertical coordination is an example.*
	• Setting up clear goals, committing to them (2)	*You have to think first about specifically what is your goal. If has to be very, very, clear. You need to have a very, very clear vision of what it is exactly that you're trying to accomplish.*

obscure locations. In addition, the sources for novel ideas and the best practices must now be sought from and deployed across a greater number of foreign affiliates, while new competitive threats are emerging throughout the world. The interview data largely supports this view. Important pressures are being placed on companies to develop executives who can comprehend the world without being excessively biased by their national origins.

3.2 Clarifying the domain of international attention

Definitions. The insights that emerge from the field interviews are generally consistent with the relevant literature on global mindset. Specifically, respondents often define international attention in terms of an outward thinking ability that allows executives to break-free of geography when processing signals from the world's environment. For many, international attention refers to the capacity to attend to important sources of ideas, regardless of where such ideas originate on the globe. As Robert Hedley, Vice President Leadership Development at Maple Leaf Foods, notes:

> You have to get your head out of the sand. You have to be looking up and out. You have to understand the marketplace better. You have to know what's going on throughout the world.

An important idea expressed by some of the respondents is that international attention involves not just outward thinking, but holistic thinking as well. Having an international focus means putting world markets and company matters into perspective and acting on them, simultaneously if need be, for the best short and long-run interests of the company. Managers with international attention were described by respondents as having the ability to hold the whole world, as it were, in their heads. They do not think about globalization as a sequential process of methodically looking at Country A, then Country B, then Function C. On the contrary, their attention practices and behaviors suggest a parallel process that looks at everything relevant more or less simultaneously. Steven Houck, Vice President of Worldwide Sales at Corel Corp, observes:

> Everyone is aware that there are markets all over the world that interact with one another. International attention is rather

archaic if it implies only that you recognize the world market. That is only one step. You must then realize that it is not one world market, but a number of markets in a global environment. It's much like religions that are successfully spread around the world. There are different dialects and ceremonies, but with a common thread of sameness.

The interview data collected echo Govindarajan and Gupta's (2001: 111) idea that a global mindset involves the ability (1) to differentiate between multiple aspects of a firm's environment (e.g. recognize similarities and differences existing across cultures and markets) and (2) to synthesize or integrate across this diversity. In addition, the interviews also reflect the perspective found in cognitive psychology literature that conceives of knowledge structures with high differentiation and integration attributes as capable of providing social actors with a greater capacity for "complicated" understanding and, more generally, an increased ability to undertake complex attention tasks (Bartunek, Gordon, & Weathersby, 1983; Weick, 1979: 261).

Operationalization. Consistent with the research objectives of this research, follow-up questions were then used to elicit categories of factors that may be normally associated with international attention. From the interviews, it appears that top executives who spend considerable time and effort thinking carefully about important international issues typically demonstrate the following set of behaviors:

(1) They use *scanning activities* to collect and analyze factual data on world markets;
(2) They *communicate and build relationships* with key constituencies worldwide, principally to acquire tacit sources of knowledge and expertise;
(3) They *use executive committee meetings* to integrate factual and tacit sources of world knowledge into a company's decision-making process.

These categories of behaviors will now be discussed in detail.

Using scanning activities to collect and analyze factual data on world markets. Several respondents indicated that having international attention means being able to actively monitor foreign exchange rates, assess host-country government regulations, and more generally, keep a close eye on all events that have possible implications for a firm's multinational network. This "active" monitoring implies careful environmental analysis by senior executives. Some respondents emphasized that the executives who are the most globally-oriented often check the validity of their assumptions by using information analysts, expert systems, business intelligence software, and/or various benchmarking techniques. Acknowledging the importance of such monitoring techniques, Chris Trojanowski, Chief Strategy Officer at Accelio, concludes:

> When I think of international attention, I think of the need to do a proper environmental scan. We actively monitor the business and market environments in different regions. We look at all business trends and currency fluctuations, and try to assess what the impact will be on our business results. We use business intelligence software to analyze customer data along a variety of different factors. Based on this data, we make decisions that support our business objectives.

Communicating and building relationships with key constituencies worldwide to acquire tacit sources of knowledge and expertise. As the interviews progressed, it became increasingly clear that senior executives with international attention also engage in frequent and dense communication exchanges with important actors worldwide (e.g. overseas managers, customers, competitors, and government officials) in order to gain first-hand information on the issues that matter the most. For instance, Chris Trojanowski, Chief Strategy Officer at Accelio observes:

> By interacting with our leading customers in foreign countries, we learn a lot about the intricacies of global markets. We get a better understanding of what business model is needed in each country. To use one example, one of our large customers is Fuji-Xerox. We meet with their management team on a quarterly basis. We try to build a relationship with these people through interaction.

This observation echoes an assumption found in international management literature that suggests that much of the world knowledge that managers need to acquire is sticky, meaning, subtle, poorly codified, and thus, difficult to transfer in pre-packaged forms. Understanding the intricacies of global markets requires constant communication exchanges and interactions. Only through this attention overtime can executives "creep into the minds of people" (Doz et al., 2001: 120) in order to comprehend issues that are pivotal to the effective functioning of an MNE. Michael Gould, Vice President of Marketing at Husky Injection Molding Systems, made the following observation:

> We must try to have a view of the world, but it is often difficult to forecast and establish what is happening in local markets, let alone remote economies. But we have different demands from different customers around the world. We need to go out and see them. We need to have a world-view of how our products and equipment are used. We need to understand what is important to different customer bases. By looking at how people behave and how they do things, we come back with a wealth of ideas that we can use in all of our markets.

In talking about the need to communicate, interact, and build relationships with key constituencies worldwide, the respondents emphasized the importance of foreign travel (face-to-face meetings), and also recognized the role of complementary media avenues such as teleconferencing and video-conferencing. The following quote from Geoff Martin, President of CCL Label at CCL Industries, illustrates this viewpoint:

> One of the important behaviors associated with international attention is to travel a lot. There are some cases of large companies in the US with operations all around the world and their people never relocate there. But in companies that are well-run, top management is constantly on the road, visiting all of these locations.
>
> Nevertheless, the next big thing for us will be video-conferencing. Business travel only makes sense if you make multiple sales calls or meetings. If it is one hour, for one customer, there is no point in flying halfway around the world. At the same time, videoconferencing is not intended to replace face-to-face contact. It is meant to

enhance or increase the contact. Normally, I would meet a certain customer as part of a much longer trip. By using videoconferencing, I can disassociate this personal interaction from physically being there, but I can still meet this customer later, when I am actually there.

Interestingly, all respondents insisted that the Chief Executive Officer (CEO) must play a critical role in this relationship-building process. Because the CEO has an integrative function in a company's top management group, and because this position represents a company's highest authority, the amount of time that a CEO spends traveling every year in foreign countries appears to be a key indicator of the extent to which the rest of a company's top management team is also paying careful attention to international issues. Guy Dupuis, Executive Vice President of Product Services at Cognos, notes:

Our CEO travels quite a bit across the various geographies in order to listen to the feedback of our global customers and to bring back important issues to us. He basically tells us what things need to be improved, issues he wants us to address. He is also very much involved in quarterly business reviews that are done throughout various geographies like Europe and Asia.

Using executive committee meetings to integrate factual and tacit sources of world knowledge into a company's decision-making process. Several respondents noted that the use of scanning activities and communication tools alone does not guarantee, by itself, the globalization of managerial attention, especially at higher levels of an organization hierarchy. For example, a new promising technology that has been developed in Japan may fail to reach the attention of a company's top team unless Japanese issues are put on the agenda of executive committee meetings. The field interviews suggest that executive committee meetings offer critical opportunities for discussing and debating those issues that emerge throughout the world, and that are deemed most important to a company's objectives. As Michel Jacques, Director Corporate Development of Alcan, observes:

Alcan's executive management team meets every month. That's the top 10–12 people in the company. They will review what we

call the top stakeholders' issues, the things that are most important to the company. They will spend most of their time talking
about top issues throughout the world, along with ongoing initiatives. They will assess how we are doing against the objectives.
They will identify emerging or outstanding issues. They will
discuss economic conditions, changes in the economic environments, changes in the exchange rates, etc....

As discussed by Ocasio (1997), such meetings constitute a type of
procedural and communication channel. According to Stinchcombe
(1968), the spatial and procedural characteristics of these channels
collectively determine and reveal what issues capture the attention
of the channels' participants. Consistent with this view, a number
of respondents suggested that it is important to consider the extent
to which

(1) major globalization decisions are subject to intensified debate;
(2) executive meetings are rotated across country locations; and
(3) multinational speakers are invited to executive meetings.

Collectively, these indicators determine whether, and to what
extent, *factual and tacit sources of world knowledge* are integrated into
a company's decision-making process. The following insights, from
Tom Jakubowski, Vice President Strategic Planning at Maple Leaf
Food, illustrate this view:

> Significant thrusts in terms of international strategy would be
> debated at the executive council level. There would be multiple
> people involved in major globalization decisions. Naturally,
> the presidents of the various divisions would be intimately
> involved in the nature of our global strategy and timing. But
> they would not be making those decisions exclusively, unto
> themselves.
>   We also want to learn from experts with international market-
> place experience. What better way can you learn about interna-
> tional issues than to talk to experts in that field? There would
> have been a fair bit of upfront analysis and investigation at the
> corporate level, as well as debate at Maple Leaf's annual strategy
> forums.

Synthesis and commentary. From the preceding discussion, and as illustrated in Figure 3-1, it is suggested that international attention is determined by the extent to which top team members (1) use scanning activities to collect and analyze factual data on world markets; (2) communicate and build relationships with key constituencies worldwide, principally to acquire tacit sources of knowledge and expertise; and (3) use executive committee meetings to integrate factual and tacit sources of world knowledge into a company's decision-making process. Taken together, these categories of attention determine an overall focus that reveals the extent to which MNE top executives allocate time, effort, and energy to international issues in their decision-making activities. Therefore, from this analysis it makes substantive sense to operationalize international attention as a formative construct (Bollen & Lennox, 1991) that is formed by a selected categories of behaviors.

As attention is selective, the construct of international attention can be conceptualized as one of degree, which falls on a continuum. At the high extreme of the continuum, top team members engage substantial time and energy in global scanning activities to pick up early warnings of opportunities and threats

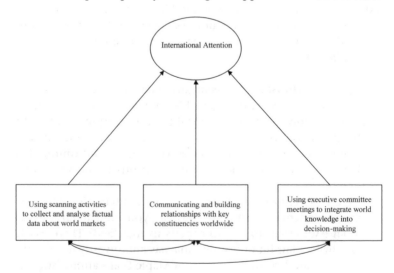

Figure 3-1 International Attention: A Formative Construct

around the world, and to better anticipate the pace and direction of future trends. They make an explicit effort to communicate regularly with key constituencies worldwide in order to further their understanding of the issues that matter the most. As well, they create room for important globalization topics on the strategic agenda of executive committee meetings. At the low extreme of the continuum, few attempts are made to stay on top of issues that fall outside managers' comfort zone. Key developments around the world can still be noticed, but only when they constitute sudden deviations from the familiar. An example of such attention-directing mechanisms would be a political coup in one of the company's major country markets, an unexpected but nevertheless attention grabbing event.

Unit of analysis. The field interviews also provided important insights on the unit of analysis that was most appropriate for understanding, conceptualizing and measuring attention to international issues. Respondents sometimes suggested that potentially all employees in a company are (or should be) concerned with foreign sources of ideas and events. For example, Pierre Ouellette, Vice President Leadership and Organizational Development at Bombardier, contends:

> I think everyone should have this global mindset. And I should say this systemic mindset. All employees should understand that we operate within a system where any decision that we make will have an impact somewhere else. Everyone should have this global perspective on things.

Nevertheless, the large majority of respondents observed that the need for international attention is highest at the top team level of analysis. The following passages illustrate this viewpoint.

- Adriana Stadecker, Director of Human Resources at Invensys:

> Not everybody needs to think global. It depends where you are in the company. Those who need international attention include the top management team, managing directors, and staff that deal with worldwide responsibilities. More and more because of technology, we are creating worldwide businesses. Therefore more people need to care about what's going on throughout the world.

- Geoff Tudhope, Vice President of Organization Development at ICI:

  We want the CEOs and Strategic Business Units heads to have international attention. In many cases, we also need it for global technology platforms and global account managers. But in our business, 20 percent of our customer base is global, and 80 percent is local. And most people can't handle the complexity of globalization. Keep it simple for 80 percent of the people.

Consistent with this view, and lessons gleaned from the economics of attention in Chapter 2, this research focuses upon the concept of attention at the top team level of analysis. The next section draws on the literatures of attention and international management, and supplements it with findings from the field interviews to develop a series of research hypotheses that will be tested in subsequent chapters. International attention is the focal construct in this framework, whose purpose is to answer two questions: (1) what factors explain international attention? And (2) what is the relationship between international attention and MNE performance?

3.3 Theory development

Figure 3-2 illustrates the conceptual framework for this research, which is comprised of four theoretical links. First, it argues that international attention is shaped primarily by the international content of an MNE's attention structures, micro-level processes that regulate the salience and legitimacy of issues that originate in distant locations (link *a*). For example,

Prahalad and Doz (1987) argue that MNEs can shape the content of data management tools, motivation schemes, and human resource development systems to promote a clear worldwide perspective within a top team. The international content of such attention structures, in turn, is affected by signals from the global environment of decisions (link *b*). These signals also impact attention allocation (link *c*), but because of the oversupply of information and the scarcity of attention, this link is only effective when the appropriate attention structures are in place. Stated more formally, this research hypothesizes that attention structures will partially mediate the relationship between the

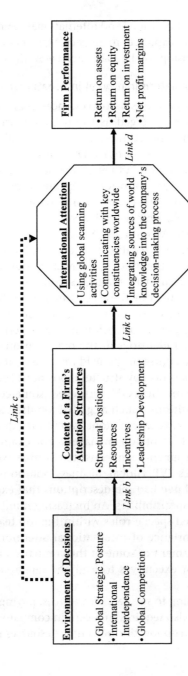

Figure 3-2 Conceptual Framework

Firm Performance
- Return on assets
- Return on equity
- Return on investment
- Net profit margins

Link d

International Attention
- Using global scanning activities
- Communicating with key constituencies worldwide
- Integrating sources of world knowledge into the company's decision-making process

Link a

Content of a Firm's Attention Structures
- Structural Positions
- Resources
- Incentives
- Leadership Development

Link b

Environment of Decisions
- Global Strategic Posture
- International Interdependence
- Global Competition

Link c

global environment of decisions and international attention. Finally, attention focusing is expected to impact MNE performance. The nature of this relationship will be elaborated below (link *d*).

Link *a*: The structural determination of international attention

The role of structural positions, resources, incentives, and leadership development activities emerged as the most important variables for fostering a global mindset. Interviewees repeatedly emphasized the powerful impact that such tools have on the behaviors of top team members, especially when they are considered as part of a total system. Each of these attention focusing roles is discussed below, in relation to Ocasio (1997) and to international management literature (Murtha et al., 1998; Prahalad & Doz, 1987).

Structural positions. According to March and Olsen (1976), attention allocation represents a rational choice that is driven by the sense of duty and obligation that stems from an individual's official role in an organization. Top managers commit their time and energy to certain tasks because these tasks are part of their job. Their structural positions become a form of cognitive filter which results in managers paying greater attention to issues germane to their obligations and social identities in the organization (Deaborne & Simon, 1958). In the course of the field interviews, it became clear that top team members occupy structural positions that necessitate a global perspective on things. Nevertheless, some companies use formal structural positions – such as global job titles and responsibilities – in order to make international attention a duty implicit to the roles and identities of top managers. For example, in 2001 Compaq's top management team consisted of nine executives: two had global job titles (VP Global Business Solutions, VP Global Business Units), and five had job descriptions that explicitly mentioned worldwide responsibilities. An increasing number of companies have also created special roles within the top team to further emphasize the importance of international attention. This move includes the appointment of some of the company's most capable and respected senior executives to lead and champion the firm's globalization efforts.

Resources. According to several interviewees, paying attention to international issues also requires that certain company resources be deployed in order to support this objective. Resources refer to those tangible and intangible assets that are utilized by a top team to accomplish critical MNE tasks (Wernerfelt, 1984). One resource that is important in the context of this study is the quality of an MNE's information infrastructure (Ghoshal & Kim, 1986). Ill-conceived email systems and corporate intranets constitute strong obstacles to corporate scanning efforts (Passino & Severance, 1990). Conversely, international attention may be promoted when an MNE's information infrastructure makes it easy for top executives to communicate and share relevant insights and expertise throughout an entire company. A quote from Donald Lang, President and CEO of CCL Industries, illustrates this viewpoint:

> What we need to have is a connected organization, and the communication tools for people to work together. You need to be able to use a corporate intranet to access common sets of information about every aspect of your business. If you have people all over the world, you need to be able to tap in and understand what is going on, without someone at the center managing it.

Incentives. The respondents also suggested that the economic and symbolic trade-off associated with competing attention claims (March & Olsen, 1976) represents an important consideration. Burgelman, among others, argues that a company's top managers typically evaluate strategic proposals "in the light of the reward and measurement systems that determine whether it is in their interest to provide impetus for a particular project" (1983: 64). This argument suggests that top team members will be more likely to pay attention to international strategic issues if they receive material rewards, social status, and credits in this process. The following observation, from Adriana Stadecker, Director of Human Resources at Invensys, is representative of the ideas that surfaced in the interviews:

> Only a minority of our people wants to think global for pure interest sake. Most have it because of the career rewards or direct accountability. I am very cynical about people doing it because it is the "right" thing to do. Unless they are rewarded-and for some people the reward is keeping their jobs-they won't pay much attention to international issues.

Several executives suggested that international attention could be achieved through the use of performance evaluation schemes and compensation systems that tie the contribution of top executives to a company's global profits and performance. The role of such economic incentives is reflected in the global mindset literature (Murtha et al., 1998). The majority of the interviewees, however, indicated that the most powerful incentives are often more symbolic in nature. Chris Trojanowski, Chief Strategy Officer at Accelio, illustrates this viewpoint in the following passage:

> In our organization, the incentive systems are not always explicit, but often implicit. For example, it is very difficult to become a vice-president if you don't have the necessary international experience. It is not written down anywhere, but you most definitely need it.

The role of symbolic incentives for fostering international attention is reflected in the literature. They consist, for example, of publicly celebrating global role models (Black et al., 1999b), linking career paths to the acquisition of international experience (Maisonrouge, 1983; Perlmutter, 1969), and ensuring that globalization is viewed as a meaningful concept that is central to a company's vision and strategic priorities (Bartlett & Ghoshal, 1994).

Leadership development. Virtually all interviewees indicated that leadership development activities may also have a strong role to play in shaping attention behaviors. This perception is based on the idea that international issues often originate in distant locations, making them difficult to comprehend without prior relevant exposure. Thus, these international issues may never be detected by insufficiently trained MNE managers (Adler & Bartholomew, 1992). Guy Dupuis, Vice President Product Services at Cognos, addresses this point:

> Developing international attention is an educational process. It is about exposing people to the things that are happening from a global perspective. It is really an educational process.

Table 3-6 provides relevant field examples of leadership development activities as they apply to the concept of international attention. These activities are consistent with a number of studies that highlight

Table 3-6 Leadership Development Activities

Mechanisms	Examples of Matching Recording Units
Company seminars and training programs	*Six times a year, we bring senior level managers together into an International Management Seminar. Our priority is to ask ourselves: How can we exchange knowledge? How can we work across borders, not only geographic borders but also cultural borders, business borders? How can we leverage the expertise developed in aerospace, but also in Transportation and Recreational Products? We decided to focus our leadership development around the globalization idea, around leveraging the group's different competencies, and making sure they are transferred from place to place.* *We focus our training initiatives around the globalization idea. We have developed a computer simulation where senior managers actually have to manage a change initiative within an organization from a multi-site, a multi-cultural, i.e. a multi-national perspective. So we bring essential skills slowly but surely into their work and their training and development so that they have this global mindset. It is a long process to reinforce these mindsets.*
International assignments	*Most of the way we address international attention is by putting people in SBU leadership positions who have worked in two or more regions around the world. They must have at least 2 years in each region in meaningful assignments. JCI has a deliberate policy of building global mindsets and has been doing this for 20 years.* *Management has to have a comfort level. Back in the mid eighties, most Canadian companies did not want to look at the US. They saw it as too competitive, too unknown, just as many markets around the world. You have to get out-there. Managers who have been on international assignments have this comfort level.*
Cross-border business teams	*Different companies have different approaches. Many things that we do, such as competitive analysis or market research, is based on the concept of virtual teams. Such teams can be cross-functional and/or cross-geographical. It is a dotted-line relationship. You could say that this is a "cloud" organization. There are no physical reporting structures, and the virtual teams are rapidly created and dissolved. Usually they have a specific task to perform, and when they are done these tasks, we create a new one. Virtual teams are very typical of global organizations.*

Table 3-6   Leadership Development Activities – *continued*

Mechanisms	Examples of Matching Recording Units
Job rotations across countries	*We like the idea of moving people around to expose them to things they can't read about in a book. We drop them into a given environment. Beyond the technical knowledge they go out and socialize. They understand the good things and the bad things, the social aspect of behavior, the culture, and why people act the way they do in a social setting.*

the role of international assignments for inculcating the skills and knowledge that routinize global thinking (Black et al., 1999a; Carpenter, Sanders, & Gregersen, 2001; Daily et al., 2000). Other leadership development activities include formal executive training programs, participation in cross border business teams, job rotations across countries, as well as various types of mentoring programs. All of these activities can be designed to shape the global leadership skills of top team members, to increase their cultural sensitivity, and to force them to forge critical relationships in various parts of the world (Black et al., 1999b; Gupta & Govindarajan, 2002).

Research hypotheses

As a result of the preceding discussion, this research proposes that the structures and systems that a company implements to channel attention towards certain activities, and away from others, constitute key determinants of attention to international issues. Specifically, the following Hypothesis is put forward:

> **Hypothesis 1:** The greater the international content of the MNE's attention structures, the greater the level of international attention in the top management team.

Link *b*: The global environment of decisions and attention structures

The global environment of decisions refers to the myriad of issues that impinge upon the decision-making activities of an MNE. This research focuses on three key variables that have received the greatest emphasis in international management literature. The first two measures relate to MNE strategy: global strategic posture (Carpenter & Fredrickson, 2001) and the level of international operational interdependence (Roth, 1995). The third measure is concerned with the level of international competition in an MNE's industry (Birkinshaw et al., 1995; Hout et al., 1982. This research suggests that all three variables send signals that reinforce the importance and legitimacy of adopting the type of attention structures described earlier.

Global strategic posture. All interviewees observed that the international content of an MNE's attention structures is likely to be largely dependent upon the company's current concept of strategy. One element of this strategy is referred to as an MNE's global strategic posture (GSP). GSP is the degree to which an MNE depends on foreign sales and foreign-placed resources (assets and employees), and the extent to which its sales and resources are geographically dispersed (Carpenter & Fredrickson, 2001). Structures that encourage managers to spread attention across multiple country locations are of limited value in companies whose strategic activity is domestically con-centrated. In these cases, attention structures may be better used to encourage other types of behaviors, such as increasing production quality, customer service, or diversity in the workplace. Other things being equal, the greater the importance of overseas sales and resources in an MNE's total activities, the greater the benefits that are derived from adopting attention structures that support international atten-tion. Thus, a company's GSP is seen as a key actor impacting the choice of structural positions, resources, incentives, and leadership development activities within an MNE.

International interdependence. While the configuration of world-wide activities (as measured by global strategic posture) is a key dimen-sion of an MNE's global strategy, several interviewees also emphasized that it is equally important to consider the level of coordination or interdependence that exists between them. International interdepend-ence is the degree to which an MNE's value-added activities (Porter, 1986) are coordinated across geographically dispersed country loca-tions (Roth, 1995). When international interdependence is low (as in multi-domestic strategies), the need for the type of globally oriented structural positions, information resources, incentives, and leadership development is limited. Conversely, the need for such attention struc-tures increases substantially when competitive advantage is based on an MNE's capacity to function as an integrated whole, with extensive coordination of value-added activities across country locations (Black et al., 1999b; Roth, 1995).

International competition. Notwithstanding the importance of an MNE's existing strategy considerations, industry dynamics can also impact the selection of attention structures. Globalization often reflects the efforts of MNEs to achieve legitimacy with other industry participants (Birkinshaw et al., 1995; Hamel & Prahalad, 1985). Thus, specific categories of attention structures are likely to be selected when considered appropriate in a given industry context (March & Olsen, 1976: 44). This condition is referred to as "structural equivalence" or "isomorphism" (DiMaggio & Powell, 1983). Moreover, because the presence of global competitors within an MNE's industry requires top managers to "pit one multinational's entire worldwide system of product and market positions against another's" (Hout et al., 1982), increasing levels of international competition should, all things being equal, motivate the adoption of attention structures that facilitate the emergence of international attentional behaviors. As a result of the above discussion, the following Hypothesis is put forward in an attempt to relate characteristics of an MNE's environment of decisions to the structuring of organizational practices:

Hypothesis 2: Attention structures are affected by the MNE's environment of decisions. Specifically, the greater the MNE's global strategic posture, international interdependence, and level of international competition, the greater the global content of an MNE's attention structures.

Link c: The environment of decisions and international attention

While the connection between the global environment of decisions and international attention is real, it is also modeled as being imperfect. Because of the oversupply of information and the scarcity of attention, an MNE's global strategic posture, the international interdependence of its operations, and the degree of international competition prevailing within its industry only have limited direct effects on international attention. While the MNE's environment of decisions drives attention processing, it does so not by itself but through its impact on the structuring of organizational practices (Ocasio, 1997). In other words, indicators of international activity in an MNE's environment of decisions constitute mental constructs that are enacted by the top team (Weick, 1979). These constructs exert an impact on the focusing of time and effort conditional upon the presence or absence of appropriate attention structures. This situation explains why organizations that belong to similar industries, or that pursue relatively comparable types of global strategies, may not pay attention to the same things. In more formal terms, this situation can be described by a partial mediation Hypothesis:

Hypothesis 3: The global content of an MNE's attention structures will mediate the relationship between the MNE's environment of decisions and the international attention of top executives.

Link *d*: International attention and MNE performance

The effective management of MNEs requires that top team members attend to important issues throughout the world (Bartlett & Ghoshal, 1989; Govindarajan & Gupta, 2001). This attention may allow them to increase their collective understanding of how operations and activities located in many different countries contribute to an overall multinational network (Athanassiou & Nigh, 2000). International attention also helps identify and leverage the ideas and the best practices that MNEs need to acquire. Tacit knowledge about an MNE's international operations and environments is not available in prepackaged forms (Doz et al., 2001), but is accumulated through personal attention over time (Winter, 1987). Finally, international attention also contributes to effective strategy execution by signaling to subsidiary managers that the corporate center is sincere in its attempt to reach informed strategic decisions that maximize the interests of all participants within an MNE's network (Kim & Mauborgne, 1993).

Despite the benefits, the opportunity cost of attention must also be considered. When scarce amounts of attention are globalized, time may be wasted looking at issues that are not important compared to other priorities at home. Moreover, as cultures are crossed and as geographical distances increase, the ability to effectively understand customers, governments, and markets becomes hampered (Gomes-Mejia & Palich, 1997; Hofstede, 1980). Thus, while the apparent fragmentation of top management's attention across multiple country locations suggests that the world is under constant review, depth of understanding may suffer, and traditional sources of competitive advantage may be put at risk. Finally, excessive levels of international attention may bring hesitation and awkwardness to an MNE's global operations (Nelson & Winter, 1982). When too much time and effort are spent thinking about worldwide developments, decision-making can become subject to inertia, or paralysis by extinction (Langley, 1995). In light of these conditions, the following argument can be hypothesized:

Hypothesis 4: There will be a curvilinear (inverted U) relationship between international attention and MNE performance.

3.4 Summary

This chapter drew upon attention theory, the relevant literature, and the qualitative insights of 18 in-depth field interviews to accomplish three research objectives. First, the practical relevance of the research questions examined in this book was verified by exploring the types of issues that currently preoccupy MNE top executives. And as expected, most companies put globalization matters at the forefront. Second, the domain of international attention was highlighted by identifying categories of behaviors that globally oriented executives normally demonstrate in their decision-making activities. Third, it provided a conceptual framework that maps the antecedents and performance implications of international attention. The theory developed in this chapter suggests that the focusing of time and effort by managers is best explained by micro-level structures – the structural positions, resources, incentives, and leadership development activities that a firm puts in place to channel attention towards certain activities and away from others. Finally, a curvilinear, inverted U-shaped relationship was hypothesized to link international attention and the overall performance of a firm. The next chapter explains the methods used to examine the statistical validity of this conceptual framework, through a cross-national mail survey of medium and large MNEs.

4
Methodology for the Quantitative Research

This chapter outlines the methodology used to test the research's hypotheses. The chapter splits naturally into two sections. The first section provides details about the sample selection process, including the choice of a multi-industry setting and the random selection of companies according to minimum size criteria. This section also provides a brief description of the main data collection instrument (mail questionnaire). The second section discusses the operationalization of the research variables.

4.1 Sample selection process

Thirteen industries (building products, chemicals, communications equipment, computers, containers and packaging, food products, industrial machinery, metals, motor vehicles and parts, pharmaceuticals, scientific instruments, semiconductors, and software) and 6 countries (USA, Canada, France, Germany, UK and Japan) were selected as the basis for the sample. Research has verified important levels of international activity that each industry and country in the sample possessed (Bartlett & Ghoshal, 1989; Birkinshaw et al., 1995; Roth, 1995). The choice of a multi-industry setting allowed the identification of enough companies in each of the selected countries for reducing the number of industries would have drastically reduced the number of participating companies in countries other than the U.S. and Japan. Apart from these practical considerations, the choice of a multi-industry setting was also consistent with the view that global mindsets have become important in a wide range of industry contexts (Doz et al., 2001; Gupta & Govindarajan, 2001; Jeannet, 2000).

A random sample of 900 MNEs was identified through *Compustat* and *Global Vantage*. The sample included MNEs that controlled and managed activities or production assets located in at least two countries (Caves, 1996) and that realized more than $US 25 million in sales. Contact information was obtained from a variety of archival sources including *Hoover's Online, Dun and Bradstreet* handbooks, the *Directory of American firms Operating in Foreign Countries*, and the *Japanese Company Handbook*, a publication of *Toyo Keizei*. Questionnaires were mailed to the CEOs or Presidents of the companies selected. To reduce the problems associated with measurement error, the survey was pre-tested with the same executives who participated in the field interviews discussed in Chapter 3. The feedback and suggestions they provided were used to eliminate or modify some of the initial items, while also adding other questions to the pool. The final instrument was mailed to the CEOs or Presidents of the companies selected in the fall of 2001. Because the implementation of follow-up procedures consistently results in increased response rates, four carefully spaced contacts were initiated with each of the respondents: (1) a pre-notification letter, (2) a questionnaire mail-out, (3) a first replacement questionnaire, and (4) a second replacement questionnaire. In total, 140 completed questionnaires were received, of which 4 were deemed not usable because of excessive missing data. Thus, the effective response rate was 15 percent (136/900). This response rate compares favorably with other cross-national mail surveys of senior executives in diversified firms (Harzing, 2000).

A single informant was used for each of the companies sampled in this study. Although the use of multiple informants can reduce concerns about possible response biases (Kumar, Stern, & Anderson, 1993), informants also have to be knowledgeable about their MNE and its international competitive environment, and be familiar with the type of structures and systems that regulate the attention of top executives. In a large cross-national sample study, identifying and obtaining accurate responses from multiple and well-informed informants is difficult to achieve. When multiple respondents are surveyed, researchers also face the risk of using informants that occupy positions that do not exist in all organizations, and increase the probability that MNEs will decline participation in the study (Doty, Glick, & Huber, 1993). The key methodological solution in using a single respondent approach is to ensure that the most knowledgeable informant in each organization is in fact providing data. Consistent with established practices in the field (Capron, 1999; Garg, Walters, & Priem, 2003; Shortell & Zajac, 1990), individuals who held a CEO or equivalent position, or had been involved as senior managers responsible for their company's worldwide efforts were assumed to be reliable key informants for this study.

4.2   Measurement

International attention

Consistent with the operational definitions provided in Chapter 3, the overarching attention construct was measured as an additive of three separate categories of behaviors that collectively reveal how top team members allocate information processing capacity, time, and effort in their decision-making activities: (1) using scanning activities to collect and analyze factual data on world markets, (2) communicating and building relationships with key constituencies worldwide to acquire tacit sources of knowledge and expertise, and (3) using executive committee meetings to integrate factual and tacit sources of world knowledge into their company's decision-making process.[1]

Attentional behaviors, Category #1: Using scanning activities to collect and analyze factual data on world markets. This was measured as the straight average of responses to a four-item reflective scale (Cronbach Alpha = 0.71) developed from global scanning and expert systems literature (Ghoshal & Kim, 1986; Ghoshal & Westney, 1991; Keegan, 1974). The following items comprised the "SCANNING" measure: "top executives collect strategic information (such as market share and competitor data from around the world) in a consistent format on a regular basis;" "the data your company

---

[1] Second-order confirmatory factor analyses were also conducted using the framework provided by Bagozzi and Heatherton (1994) for modeling multifaceted constructs. The findings provide strong support for the intended factor structure, and demonstrate adequate convergent and discriminant validity.

collects from around the world is pre-filtered by information analysts before being disseminated;" "your top executives use business intelligence software to analyze global market developments;" "your top executives use benchmarking systems that routinely compare the company against key competitors worldwide." The scale used a 1–5 Likert scale format where 1 signifies "very rarely" and 5 "very frequently."

Attentional behaviors, Category #2: Communicating/building relationships with constituencies worldwide. Two separate measures were used here, MEDIA and CEO TRAVEL. MEDIA was the weighted average of responses to a four-item formative scale that was developed from the media richness literature (Daft & Lengel, 1986; Weick & Van Orden, 1990). Respondents were asked to indicate how often they use email, letters, and memos (weight of 1), the telephone (weight of 2), videoconferences (weight of 3), and/or face-to-face meetings (weight of 4) to discuss non-routine decisions with overseas managers. The weights reflect increasing intensities of attention in assessing media richness. CEO TRAVEL assessed the amount of time that a chief executive officer spends traveling abroad every year. This measure was used to evaluate the specific boundary-spanning role played by the CEO in the process of interacting with key stakeholders worldwide. This measure asked respondents to indicate how much time (in percentage) their CEO spent working at the company headquarters, traveling throughout the domestic market, and traveling outside the domestic market. In this sample, responses to the third item averaged 25 percent (s.d. = 16) with a range of 0 to 80 percent. This result indicates that 95 percent of the CEOs in the set of responding companies spent between 9 and 41 percent of their time traveling around the world every year.

Attentional behaviors, Category #3: Using executive committee meetings to integrate factual and tacit sources of world knowledge into a company's decision-making process. This category of attentional behaviors was measured as the straight average of responses to a three-item formative scale labeled "DECISION MAKING." Specifically, respondents were asked to indicate the extent to which "top management meetings are rotated across locations," "top management meetings involve speakers from multinational locations," and "major globalization decisions are made after intensive discussions between top managers." These questions used a 1–5 Likert scale format where 1 indicated "very rarely" and 5 "very frequently."

Overall composite measure: Following Nunnally and Bernstein's (1994) classification of Likert as interval data, an overall additive index of international attention was created. Indicator variables were transformed to z-scores, and the scores obtained on each variable were summed. The overall index was standardized so that its mean equals zero and standard deviation equals 1. Table 4-1 shows the correlations between the indicators and the composite measure. This table reveals that the intercorrelations between indicators are moderate, with values ranging from 0.17 to 0.46. However, each indicator has a relatively high correlation with the composite measure, suggesting it contributes a unique variance to the total index. As Epstein notes: "an ideal item in a test that measures a broad trait is one that has a relatively high correlation with the sum of all items in the test and a relatively low average correlation with the other items" (1983).

Moreover, the moderate correlations found between the scanning, media, CEO travel, and decision-making measures make substantive sense since the international attention construct was described in Chapter 3 as a latent formative construct that is formed by the selected indicators.

The optimal level of homogeneity occurs when the mean inter item correlation is in the 0.2 to 0.4 range. Lower than 0.1 and it is likely that a single total score could not adequately represent the complexity of the items; higher than 0.5 and the items on a

Table 4-1   Correlations Between Attention Variables

	Scanning	Media	CEO travel	Decision-making
Scanning	1.00			
Media	0.28	1.00		
CEO travel	0.19	0.46	1.00	
Decision-making	0.17	0.30	0.32	1.00
Composite measure	0.60	0.75	0.72	0.66

Correlations greater than 0.17 and 0.19 and are significant at the 0.05 level and 0.01 level.

scale tend to be redundant and the construct measured too specific. The 0.2 to 0.4 range of intercorrelations would seem to offer an acceptable balance between bandwidth on the one hand, and fidelity on the other (Briggs & Cheek, 1986).

Also, implicit in this operational definition is the notion that if any category of behaviors increases (e.g., the richness of communications with key constituencies worldwide), the degree to which a firm's top team has international attention increases even if the other categories of behaviors stay the same. In addition, changes in the composite measure do not require a simultaneous change in all categories of behaviors. Therefore, a reliable measure of international attention should include *all* facets. The scanning, media, CEO travel, and decision-making measures are "representative" of distinct dimensions of the latent construct, which also means they are not interchangeable. Omitting any of these indicators would result in a faulty measure since it would mean omitting part of the construct. In the following passage, Cattel summarizes this view, which emphasizes the need to consider the behavioral indicators as part of a total system rather than in isolation:

> Usually, in a well functioning machine or living organism, we judge its efficiency by how well it functions as a whole. We do not expect the parts all to be exactly the same, and indeed, such homogeneity is the mark of a lower organism. Similarly, any complex and ingenious test may need to be put together like a watch, with all its parts properly balanced for some final results. If it is chopped up the scores on its parts need not necessarily correlate highly with one another (Cattel, 1965).

The global content of a firm's attention structures

Although the four categories of attention structures discussed in this study are conceptually different, an empirical distinction between them can be difficult to achieve for they *reflect* the same macro phenomenon, i.e. a systemic attempt by an organization to increase international attention. As a result, a principal component factor analysis was performed on a 15-item reflective scale (Table 4-2, overall Cronbach Alpha = 0.87) that included various measures of attention structures (structural positions, resources, incentives, and leadership development).

Table 4-2 Exploratory Factor Analysis

Items	Symbolic Incentives	Leadership Development	Economic Incentives	Inform. Resources	Structural Positions
1. For advancement to company senior ranks, managers need substantial international experience	.72	.36	.18	.06	-.05
2. The company gives high visibility to global role models	.65	.30	.30	.10	.11
3. Globalization creates career opportunities for your managers	.71	.36	.21	.03	.15
4. The word globalization describes a concept that is central to your company's vision	.83	.06	.10	.12	.16
5. The word globalization helps everybody understand the company's priorities	.75	.16	.09	.11	.10
6. Your company uses seminars and training programs to globalize its senior managers	.22	.60	.17	.29	.07
7. Your company uses international assignments to globalize its senior managers	.41	.72	.04	.09	-.03
8. Your company uses cross-border business teams to globalize its senior managers	.39	.56	.19	.01	.06
9. Your company uses job rotations across countries to globalize its senior managers	.18	.79	-.10	.12	-.11
10. Your company uses mentoring programs countries to globalize its senior managers	.09	.73	.19	.00	.26
11. Top executives' compensation is linked to their contribution to the company's global performance	.24	.00	.87	.07	.00

Table 4-2 Exploratory Factor Analysis – continued

Items	Symbolic Incentives	Leadership Development	Economic Incentives	Inform. Resources	Structural Positions
12. Top executives' performance evaluation is tied to their contribution to the company's global profits	.43	.07	.73	.08	.11
13. Your company makes it easy for senior managers to travel internationally (e.g. everyone flies business class, the company pays high per diem for overseas trips, etc.)	.00	.32	.48	.12	.16
14. Your global Intranet provides managers an easy way to share insights and best with practices across the entire company	.08	.05	.01	.88	.18
15. Your global IT infrastructure makes it easy for executives to communicate quickly with anyone in the company	.16	.23	.20	.81	–.07
16. One or several senior executives have been asked to champion the company's globalization efforts	.08	.01	.06	–.04	.88
17. Extensive use is made of global job titles/ responsibilities – e.g. V.P. Global Sales vs. V.P. Sales	.19	.10	.10	.17	.74
Eigenvalues	6.08	1.63	1.40	1.25	1.01
% Variance explained	36	36	10	46	8
% Cumulative variance	54	7	61	6	67
Cronbach Alpha	.87	.81	.82	.72	Formative

When only considering the factors that have latent roots (eigenvalues) greater than one to be significant, the VARIMAX rotated component analysis yielded a five-factor structure that explained 67 percent of the variance in the sample. While a few variables loaded significantly (0.3) on several factors, in each case the differences between the highest loading and the next significant loadings (in italics) were great. As a result, the cross-loadings were viewed as not meaningful. Placing greater emphasis on those variables with the highest loadings (0.5 and higher), the following labels were assigned: (1) symbolic incentives, (2) leadership development, (3) economic incentives, (4) information resources, and (5) structural positions. Item number 13 was dropped due to a weak loading below 0.50, and because it had a large negative impact on the Cronbach alpha of its latent factor.

Internal reliability tests on the four factors showed adequate Cronbach alphas, whose values ranged between 0.72 and 0.87. Therefore, the VARIMAX rotated component analysis establishes both the relatedness and the conceptual separation that exists between distinct categories of attention structures. The next step was to form composite, equally weighted measures for each factor. A mean composite index of the attention structure variables was created and standardized to test the possibility of mediation effects (Hypothesis 3). Hypotheses 1 and 2 were tested using both the overall index and the four separate attention structures measures.

Table 4-3 shows the inter-correlations among attention structures. These correlations are moderate to high, with values ranging from 0.17 to 0.61. The highest correlations are observed between the symbolic incentives and leadership development variables (0.61). However, in light of the VARIMAX rotated component factor analysis two separate measures were kept for these factors.

Table 4-3   Correlations Between Attention Structures Variables

	A	B	C	D	E
A: Symbolic incentives	1.00				
B: Leadership development	.61	1.00			
C: Economic incentives	.50	.33	1.00		
D: Information resources	.31	.34	.24	1.00	
E: Structural positions	.28	.20	.24	.17	1.00

All correlations are significant at the 0.01 level.

Environment of decisions

Global Strategic Posture. This four-item scale variable was based on Sanders and Carpenter (1998). The first item gauges a firm's dependence on sales to foreign markets and is calculated as the ratio of foreign sales to total sales. The second and third items were measured by weighing foreign assets and foreign employees as a percentage to total assets and total employees respectively. These items reflect a firm's reliance on foreign-placed resources. The fourth item estimates the number of countries in which a firm operates as a percentage of the highest number of countries represented among the firms in our sample. It provides an indication of the cultural variety associated with the previous three dimensions. The indicators of foreign sales, foreign production, foreign employees, and cultural variety are summed to create a composite index of global strategic posture. A principal component factor analysis reveals that these four indicators loaded on one factor (eigenvalue = 2.4; Cronbach alpha = 0.76). Since each of the four indicators is a ratio variable ranging from 0 to 1, the composite measure can theoretically range from 0 (no international activity) to 4 (extensive global strategic posture). In this sample, global strategic posture averaged 1.37 (s.d. = 0.68), with a range of 0.16 to 3.35.

International interdependence. This variable was measured by decomposing a firm's value-chain and assessing the extent of integration/coordination across geographically dispersed locations (Roth, 1995). Eight activities were listed: raw materials/parts procurement, manufacturing, process design/improvement, marketing/sales activities, product design/improvement, finance, accounting/legal functions, and employee development. Respondents were asked to indicate whether each activity was "performed in one country," "performed in multiple countries and managed nationally," "performed in multiple countries and coordinated within regions," and "performed in multiple countries and coordinated globally." The proxy of international interdependence was obtained by summing the responses for each activity; it can range from 9 (the activities are performed in one country) to 36 (the activities are performed in multiple countries and coordinated globally). In this sample, international interdependence averaged 25.8 (s.d. = 5.89).

International competition. The presence of international competitive pressures in a firm's industry was measured with a four-item scale (Birkinshaw et al., 1995). Specifically, respondents were asked to report how characteristic each of the following statements was in regards to the most prominent industry segment in which their company competed: "International competition is intense," "Competitors exist that have a presence in all global markets," "New product introductions tend to occur in all major international markets simultaneously," and "Competitors market a standardized product worldwide." A principal component factor analysis on the four items yielded a single construct (eigenvalue of 2.743; Cronbach Alpha = 0.74). An index was computed as the mean value of the four variables, averaging 4.6 (s.d = 1.16), with a range of 1.75 to 6.5.

Performance

MNE performance was measured using five-year (1995–2001) averages of four profitability indicators: return on assets, return on equity, return on investment, and net profit margins, adjusted by industry and risk by subtracting each variable from its industry mean, and then dividing it by its standard deviation. All measures were obtained through Standard and Poor's *Compustat* and *Global Vantage* databases. Because companies present their financial results in a variety of formats, it may be difficult to make accurate and meaningful company comparisons. To mitigate this issue, the data provided by Standard and Poor is using consistent sets of financial data items that have been normalized according to local accounting principles, disclosure methods and data item definitions, thus diminishing problems of variability and bias in reporting procedures. Correlations between the five performance indicators ranged from 0.5 to 0.8. A principal component factor analysis yielded a single overarching factor, explaining 85 percent of variance. Thus, a weighted average composite measure was created in order to be included in the regressions. Descriptive statistics for performance variables are presented in Table 4-4.

Table 4-4   Industry and Risk Adjusted Performance Indicators

	Minimum	Maximum	Mean	Std. Dev.
5-year Return on Assets	–5.36	3.18	0.32	1.00
5-year Return on Equity	–6.78	3.47	0.20	1.00
5-year Return on Investments	–5.23	3.15	0.25	1.00
5-year Return on Sales	–5.93	2.56	0.19	1.00
Weighted Average Composite Measure	–11.00	5.59	–0.87	2.33

Control variables

Control variables were used to ensure that observed effects were not due to unmeasured confounding factors. Data on the controls was obtained through archival sources, including *Compustat, Global Vantage, Hoovers*, and company web sites. Past research indicates that MNEs from different geographical regions frequently exhibit different behaviors (Bartlett & Ghoshal, 1986; Chandler, 1970). Therefore, a dummy variable was used to control for locational effects (coded 1 if the diversified firm was headquartered in the United States, and 0 otherwise). As firm size, R&D intensity, and diversification have been shown to affect various organizational outcomes (Hitt, Hoskisson, & Kim, 1997), they were included as controls. Firm size was measured as the logarithm of firm employees. Other measures of size, such as total sales and total assets, yielded similar results. R&D intensity was measured as the ratio of R&D expenses to firm sales. Firm diversification was measured using an entropy measure (Palepu, 1985):

$$\text{Diversification} = \Sigma i \left[(P_i * \ln (1/ P_i)) \right]$$

Here P_i is the sales attributed to segment i and $\ln (1/P_i)$ is the weight given to that segment over all of a firm's businesses. Similar results were obtained with other measures of diversification such as the number of two-digit or four-digit sic codes.

Top team characteristics (the size, cultural heterogeneity, and international experience of a firm's top management group) were included as controls because of their possible impact on cognition and behaviors (Hambrick & Mason, 1984). The size of the top team was measured as the number of company officers who operate at one and two levels below the CEO. Cultural heterogeneity was measured by the mix of nationalities within the top management group (Earley, 2000). And international experience was calculated as the number of company officers who have spent at least a year in a single foreign assignment (Black et al., 1999a).

5
Results

In reporting the results, the questionnaire results are interwoven with interview findings to construct a comprehensive picture of the hypotheses under study.

5.1   Hypothesis testing

For all models involving continuous dependent variables, multivariate regression techniques were used. In each case, precautionary analyses (Cook & Weisberg, 1982) indicated that outliers were not present in the database, and therefore did not exert any influential impact on the results obtained. Hierarchical analysis was used to ensure that the coefficients associated with the independent variables were stable. Variance inflation factors (VIF) and tolerances for individual variables were all within adequate parameters. Therefore, multicollinearity did not seem to threaten the estimates.

Hypothesis 1: Attention structures and attention to international issues

The first Hypothesis predicted that international attention is shaped by the content of a firm's attention structures (Figure 5-1). This Hypothesis was tested using ordinary least square (OLS) regression analysis (Table 5-1). The standardized coefficients for the control variables are shown in Model 1, where the variables for firm size, R&D intensity, and mix of nationality are significant and positively related to global mindset ($p < 0.05$). The results presented in the following models provide support to Hypothesis 1. In Model 2, the

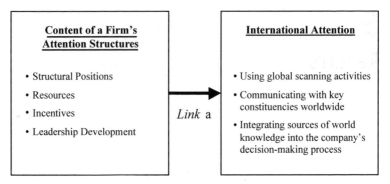

Figure 5-1   A Visual Representation of Hypothesis 1

inclusion of the term for the overall content of a firm's attention structures accounted for significant and unique variance (i.e. 39 percent) in the dependent variable.

Similar results are obtained in Models 3 to 7, where the attention structures variables are entered separately into the regression equation ($p < .05$). Here, leadership development and symbolic incentives account for the greatest proportion of variance in international attention (29 and 31 percent, respectively). The analysis provided in Model 8 reveals that the effect of structural positions is no longer significant when all categories of attention structures variables are entered into the same model. Similarly, the effect of economic incentives is weakened, remaining marginally significant at the $p < 0.10$ level. These results were robust when also controlling for the confounding effects of variables that pertain to a firm's environment of decisions (more on this later in the section on mediation Hypothesis).

Post-hoc tests. Table 5-2 provides a more fine-grained analysis of H1 by showing how attention structures individually relate to the various measures of international attention. Partial correlation coefficients were used to control for the confounding effects of firm size, R&D intensity, and cultural heterogeneity. Out of the 20 correlations in this table, 16 are statistically significant and positively signed. As well, symbolic incentives, leadership development, and economic incentives are the only categories of attention structures that are significantly and positively correlated to all four measures of global mindset. Hence, information resources and structural

Table 5-1   OLS Regression: Predicting Attention to International Issues

	International Attention – Composite Measure							
	Model 1	Model 2	Model 3	Model 4	Model 5	Model 6	Model 7	Model 8
Control Variables								
US dummy	-.11	-.09	-.18	-.09	-.17	-.01	-.09	-.07
Firm age	-.03	-.01	-.02	-.02	-.03	-.01	-.01	-.00
Firm size	.26*	.31***	.30*	.26*	.33*	.22*	.33***	.30***
R&D intensity	.21*	.23***	.19*	.17*	.27*	.23*	.22**	.23***
Diversification	-.07	-.10	-.10	-.04	-.09	-.10	-.13*	-.12
Top Team Characteristics								
Size	-.03	-.13†	-.08	-.11	-.07	-.07	-.04	-.11
International experience	.15	-.01	.15	.09	.07	.06	.04	.00
Cultural heterogeneity	.19*	.17**	.21*	.23*	.16*	.17*	.13*	.16*
Attention Structures								
Attention structures index		.63***						
Structural positions			.29***					.08
Information resources				.35***				.14*
Economic incentives					.40***			.12†
Leadership development						.56***		.27***
Symbolic incentives							.56***	.28***
Model Indices								
R^2	.23	.60	.31	.34	.38	.50	.52	.57
Adjusted R^2	.18	.57	.26	.29	.34	.47	.49	.61
Increase in Adjusted R^2		.39	.08	.11	.16	.29	.31	.38

[a] n = 136. Standardized coefficients are shown. Variance Inflation Factors values are less than 3.
† $p < 0.10$; * $p < 0.05$; ** $p < 0.01$; *** $p < 0.001$

Table 5-2   Partial Correlations Coefficients[a] (Attention Structures –
International Attention)

	Scanning	Media	CEO travel	Decision-making
Symbolic incentives	.35**	.51**	.35**	.38**
Leadership development	.38**	.51**	.27**	.40**
Economic incentives	.18*	.44**	.25**	.23**
Information resources	.44**	.27**	.13†	.16
Structural positions	.05	.24*	.16†	.23*

[a] Controlling for firm size, R&D intensity and mix of nationality
† $p < 0.10$; * $p < 0.05$; ** $p < 0.01$

positions were found to appear to exert a more limited impact on international attention.

A Multivariate General Linear Model (GLM) was used to verify that the results are robust across the various international attention measures. This statistical procedure provides regression analysis and analysis of variance for a set of multiple dependent variables. The results of the multivariate GLM model are presented in Table 5-3 (models 9A to 9D). This table indicates that the coefficient on the attention structures index is positive and significant in the case of each dependent variable. This evidence provides additional support to Hypothesis 1.

Hypothesis 2: Environment signals and attention structures

Hypothesis 2 predicted that attention structures would be affected by signals from an MNE's environment of decisions. This Hypothesis was tested by regressing the overall attention structures index on the three environment signals (Table 5-4, models 10 to 13). Model 10 contains the control variables. This model is not significant (p-value = 0.14). Model 11 adds the global strategic posture variable, whose coefficient is positive and significant, adding eleven percent of variance in the dependent variable. In Model 12, the international interdependence variable is positively and significantly related to the overall attention structures index, adding four percent of additional variance. Finally, Model 13 adds the international competition variable. The coefficient on this variable is positive and significant, with the variance explained increasing another seven percent.

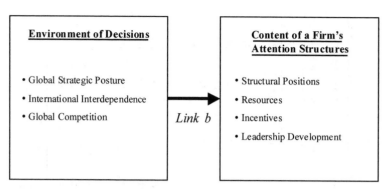

Figure 5-2   A Visual Representation of Hypothesis 2

These results support Hypothesis 2. The content of a firm's attention structures appears to be affected by signals from the environment of decisions. More specifically, the expansiveness of a firm's global strategic posture, the international interdependence of its operations, and the amount of international competition prevailing within its major industry segment contribute to explain approximately 22 percent of additional variance in the overall attention structures index, compared to the initial control model.

Post-hoc tests. A GLM multivariate procedure was used to examine the adoption of attention structures, taken as a set of multiple dependent variables (Table 5-5, models 14A to 14E). This procedure indicates that a firm's global strategic posture is positively associated with the economic and symbolic incentives variables. The other strategy dimension, which pertains to the international interdependence of a firm's operations, appears to best predict the choice of structural positions, leadership development, and symbolic incentives ($p < 0.05$). Finally, the coefficient for the international competition variable is positive and significant when leadership development and symbolic incentives are the dependent variables. Consistent with the principle of equifinality, this pattern of results indicates that firms respond to different environmental contingencies by combining together and substituting between alternative types of attention structures (structural positions, information resources, economic and symbolic incentives, and leadership development).

Table 5-3 GLM Multivariate: International Attention

	Model 9A Info		Model 9B Media		Model 9C CEO Travel		Model 9D Decision Making	
	B	S.E.	B	S.E.	B	S.E.	B	S.E.
Intercept	3.88***	.29	4.69***	.22	16.85***	3.80	3.97***	.29
Control Variables								
US dummy	-.57**	.19	.03	.15	-3.78	2.57	.14	.20
Firm age	-.00†	.00	.00	.00	-.01	.03	.00	.00
Firm size	.30***	.07	.08	.05	.09	.92	.17*	.07
R&D intensity	.01†	.00	.01	.00	.10	.06	.01**	.00
Diversification	-.28	.22	-.13	.16	2.07	2.85	-.47*	.22
Top Team Characteristics								
Size	-.02	.03	-.01	.02	-.80*	.36	-.01	.03
International experience	-.06	.04	-.01	.03	1.19*	.56	-.03	.04
Mix of nationality	-.05	.04	.03	.03	2.28***	.59	.10*	.04
Attention structures index	.57***	.09	.55***	.07	4.73***	1.21	.46***	.09
Model Indices								
F-Value	8.42		9.06		7.62		5.89	
R^2	.37		.39		.35		.30	
Adjusted R^2	.33		.35		.31		.25	

[a] $n = 136$. Un-standardized coefficients are shown. Variance Inflation Factors values are less than 3.
† $p < 0.10$; * $p < 0.05$; ** $p < 0.01$; *** $p < 0.001$

Table 5-4   OLS Regression: Content of Attention Structures

	ATTENTION STRUCTURES INDEX			
	Model 10	Model 11	Model 12	Model 13
Control Variables				
US dummy	−.03	.02	−.04	.01
Firm age	−.03	−.03	−.06	−.04
Firm size	−.07	−.15	−.19†	−.19†
R&D intensity	−.03	−.05	−.06	−.07
Diversification	.05	.02	.01	−.03
Top Team Characteristics				
Size	.15	.18†	.15	.15
Mix of nationality	.04	−.06	−.07	−.03
International experience	.24*	.16	.13	.14
Environment of Decisions				
Global strategic posture		.38***	.29**	.26**
International interdependence			.26**	.27**
International competition				.27***
Model Indices				
Significance	.14	.00	.00	.00
R^2	.09	.20	.24	.31
Adjusted R^2	.03	.14	.18	.25
Increase in Adjusted R^2	.03	.11	.04	.07

[a] n = 136. Standardized coefficients are shown. Variance Inflation Factors values are less than 3.
† $p < 0.10$; * $p < 0.05$; ** $p < 0.01$; *** $p < 0.001$

Hypothesis 3: The mediating effect of attention structures

Hypothesis 3 predicted that the content of a firm's attention structures would partially mediate the relationship between the environment of decisions, and international attention. Following the procedures described by Baron and Kenny (1986), the international attention variable was regressed on global strategic posture, international interdependence and international competition, without (step 1) and with (step 2) controlling for the attention structures index (Table 5-6).

In Model 15, the regression analysis reveals a significant coefficient (0.48) at the 0.01 level on the global strategic posture variable (step 1). However, when controlling for the attention structures index (step 2),

Table 5-5   GLM Regression: Content of Attention Structures

	Model 14A Structural Positions		Model 14B Information Resources		Model 14C Economic Incentives		Model 14D Leadership Development		Model 14E Symbolic Incentives	
	B	S.E.	B	S.E.	B	S.E.	B	S.E.	B	S.E.
Intercept	4.60***	.27	5.01***	.21	5.85***	.20	3.73***	.17	4.80***	.15
Control Variables										
US dummy	.75*	.35	-.07	.27	.48*	.25	-.49*	.22	.01	.19
Firm age	-.07	.17	-.02	.13	-.01	.12	-.05	.11	-.05	.09
Firm size	-.33	.22	-.04	.17	-.30*	.15	-.02	.13	-.30*	.12
R&D intensity	.09	.16	.13	.13	-.23*	.12	-.09	.10	-.09	.09
Diversification	.14	.16	-.16	.12	.00	.11	-.01	.10	.02	.09
Top Team Characteristics										
Size	.25	.18	.32*	.14	.11	.13	.06	.11	.02	.10
International experience	-.10	.18	.18	.14	.16	.13	.10	.11	.09	.10
Cultural heterogeneity	-.14	.17	-.17	.13	.03	.12	-.00	.10	.04	.09
Environment of Decisions										
Global strategic posture	-.05	.18	.26†	.14	.29*	.13	.13	.11	.31**	.10
International interdependence	.48*	.18	.03	.14	.17	.13	.35**	.11	.38***	.10
International competition	.14	.15	.20†	.12	.17	.11	.22*	.09	.42***	.08
Model Indices										
F-Value	2.24		2.23		2.33		3.57		7.21	
R^2	.17		.16		.17		.24		.39	
Adjusted R^2	.09		.09		.10		.17		.34	

[a] n = 136. Unstandardized coefficients are shown. Variance Inflation Factors values are less than 3.
† $p < 0.10$; * $p < 0.05$; ** $p < 0.01$; *** $p < 0.001$

Table 5-6 OLS Regression: Mediating Effect

| | International Attention – Composite Measure | | | | | |
| | Model 15 | | Model 16 | | Model 17 | |
	Step 1[b]	Step 2[b]	Step 1[b]	Step 2[b]	Step 1[b]	Step 2[b]
Control Variables						
US dummy	-.05	-.06	-.16*	-.10	-.08	-.10
Firm age	-.02	-.01	-.06	-.01	-.01	-.01
Firm size	.18†	.26**	.20†	.30***	.26*	.31***
R&D intensity	.18*	.21**	.20*	.22***	.20*	.23***
Diversification	-.10	-.11	-.09	-.10†	-.09	-.10
Top Team Characteristics						
Size	.01	-.09	-.06	-.13†	-.03	-.13†
International experience	.05	-.04	.10	-.01	.15	-.01
Cultural heterogeneity	.08	.11†	.16*	.17**	.21*	.17**
Environment of Decisions						
Global strategic posture	.45***	.24***				
International interdependence			.27**	.05		
International competition					.17*	-.02
Attention structures index		.56***		.62***		.64***
R²	.38	.63	.28	.60	.26	.60
Adjusted R²	.34	.60	.23	.56	.20	.56

[a] n = 136. Standardized coefficients are shown. Variance Inflation Factors values are less than 3.
† p < 0.10; * p < 0.05; ** p < 0.01; *** p < 0.001

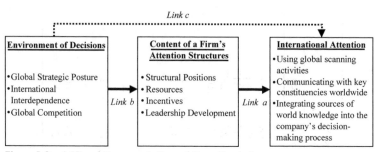

Figure 5-3   A Visual Representation of Hypothesis 3

the standardized regression coefficient drops to 0.25. Even more drastic effects were observed in Models 16 and 17, where controlling for the attention structures index makes the coefficients on the international interdependence and international competition variables no longer statistically significant.

These procedures, along with the earlier tests that established the validity of Hypotheses 1 and 2 suggest that the relationship between global strategic posture and international attention is partially mediated by the content of a firm's attention structures. With respect to the two other variables (namely international interdependence and international competition), a full mediation effect can be observed. Therefore, if signals from the environment of decisions affect attentional processing within a top team, this relationship appears to be largely imperfect and dependent upon the content of a firm's attention structures. This evidence provides support for Hypothesis 3.

Hypothesis 4: Performance Implications of a global mindset

Hypothesis 4 predicted that the effect of international attention is curvilinear with respect to firm performance. This Hypothesis was tested using ordinary least square regression analysis (Table 5-7). Model 18 includes all control variables. This model is significant at the 0.01 level. In Model 19, the international attention variable was not significantly related to firm performance, its inclusion adding only 1.2 percent to the variance explained by the control model. Model 20 provides a direct test of Hypothesis 4 by adding a square term for the international attention variable. The coefficient on the square term was significant and negatively signed ($p < 0.05$), explaining 2.7 percent of additional variance. The coefficient on

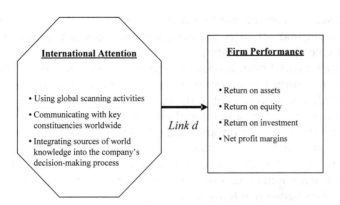

Figure 5-4   A Visual Representation of Hypothesis 4

Table 5-7   OLS Regression: Firm Performance[a]

	Model 18		Model 19		Model 20	
	B	S.E	B	S.E	B	S.E
Intercept	−.50	.64	−.60	.65	−.44	64
Control Variables						
US dummy	1.07*	.43	1.00*	.43	.96*	.43
Firm age	.00	.00	.00	.00	.00	.00
Firm size	.17	.15	.21	.16	.25	.15
R&D intensity	−.02*	.01	−.02*	.01	−.02	.01
Diversification	−.15	.47	−.20	.47	−.15	.47
Top Team Characteristics						
Size	−.15*	.06	−.16*	.06	−.15*	.06
International experience	.07	.09	.09	.09	.10	.09
Cultural heterogeneity	−.02	.10	.01	.10	−.01	.10
International attention index			−.29	.22	−.33	.22
International attention squared					−.29*	.15
Model Indices						
F-Value	2.59		2.50		2.72	
R^2	.14		.15		.18	
Adjusted R^2	.09		.09		.11	

[a] $n = 136$. Unstandardized coefficients are shown. Variance Inflation Factors values are less than 3.
† $p < 0.10$; * $p < 0.05$; ** $p < 0.01$; *** $p < 0.001$

the simple term was not significant and negatively signed. Keeping in mind that the international attention index is a standardized variable that takes both positive and negative values, this test reveals a curvilinear, inverted U relationship (Aiken & West, 1991: 66). Therefore, the regression analysis results reported in Table 5-7 provide statistical support to Hypothesis 4.

Figure 5-5 offers a graphic display of the association between international attention and firm performance. Performance was evaluated at the mean values of each variable entered into the regression, when the US dummy was coded 1, for varying levels of the international attention variable. Figure 5-5 indicates the relationship between international attention and firm performance. This relationship is initially positive at lower levels of the international attention variable, but as the value of this variable increases beyond the sample mean, however, firms start experiencing diminishing returns, after which negative returns set in.

Post-hoc tests. The threat of alternative specifications was examined by adding additional controls to the models. In particular, industry dummies were used to control for industry-level effects with consistent results. The possibility of reverse causality was examined by entering a term for prior performance in the equation regression. The results were robust. The international attention index was also regressed on the performance measure. The coefficient for this variable was negatively signed, and not statistically significant ($p = .193$), suggesting that

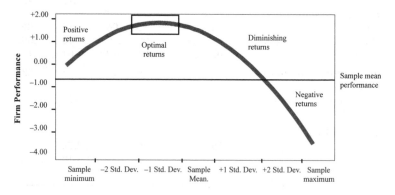

Figure 5-5   Global Mindset: A Mixed Blessing?

overall performance levels have a limited impact on the extent to which top members allocate attention to international issues.

The three variables pertaining to a firm's environment of decisions (global strategic posture, international interdependence, and international competition) were added to the regression equation, but none were found to be significantly related to firm performance. The interaction between international attention and the three environment signals was also examined to see if the expansiveness of a firm's global strategic posture, the international interdependence of its operations, and/or the degree of international competition prevailing within its industry would modify the curvilinear relationship that the international attention variable exerts on firm performance, but no significant effect was detected. Finally, the effect of the overall attention structures index on firm performance was also examined, but no such effect was found.

The relationship between attention and performance was subsequently examined using a subjective measure of firm performance that captured "effectiveness" factors that are more difficult to measure and observe using accounting numbers (Table 5-8.) In this case, the dependent variable was the straight average of responses to a three-item scale (Cronbach Alpha = 0.67) that asked respondents to indicate their company's relative performance (compared to other companies in their industry) on the following three items: "personnel development," "overall reputation as an industry leader," and "quality of products and services."

In Model 22, the international attention variable is positively and significantly related to the measure of firm effectiveness. In Model 23, the coefficient for the square attention term is not significant. Therefore, while international attention was shown to have a concave relationship with firm performance when accounting numbers were used as the dependent variable, it has linearly positive implications for firm performance when other components of firm success – such as employee development, the perceived reputation of the firm, and the quality of its products/services – are taken into account. It is also interesting to note that the coefficient for a firm's global strategic posture is significant and negatively signed (Model 24), but this effect, however, is not substantial (the addition of the term for this variable does not significantly increase the variance explained for firm effectiveness).

Table 5-8 OLS Regression: Firm Effectiveness[a]

	Model 21		Model 22		Model 23		Model 24	
	B	S.E	B	S.E	B	S.E	B	S.E.
Intercept	5.31***	.22	5.39***	.22	5.38***	.22	6.01***	.45
Control Variables								
US dummy	.25†	.15	.29*	.14	.30*	.15	.29*	.15
Firm age	-.00	.00	-.00	.00	-.00	.00	-.00	.00
Firm size	-.09	.05	-.12*	.05	-.12	.05	-.11*	.05
R&D intensity	.00	.00	.00	.00	.00	.00	-.00	.00
Diversification	-.28†	.16	-.25	.16	-.25	.16	-.18	.16
Top Team Characteristics								
Size	.05*	.02	.05*	.02	.05*	.02	.04*	.02
International experience	-.01	.03	-.02	.03	-.02	.03	-.01	.03
Cultural heterogeneity	.04	.03	.02	.03	.02	.03	.04	.03
Predictor Variables								
International attention index			.20**	.07	.20**	.07	.31***	.08
International attention squared					.01	.05	.03	.05
Environment of Decisions								
Global strategic posture							-.27*	.13
International interdependence							-.01	.01
International competition							-.02	.06
F-Value	2.90		3.56		3.1		3.05	
R^2	.15		.20		.20		.24	
Adjusted R^2	.10		.15		.14		.16	

[a] $n = 136$. Unstandardized coefficients are shown. Variance Inflation Factors values are less than 3.
† $p < 0.10$; * $p < 0.05$; ** $p < 0.01$; *** $p < 0.001$

5.2 Post-test interview results and discussion

Post-test interviews were conducted to supplement the quantitative analysis provided above. The purpose of these follow-up interviews was to enhance interpretation of the findings obtained from the questionnaire data, and to aid in identifying potentially valuable avenues for future research. An attempt was made to select a geographically diverse group of MNEs in order to minimize potential regional bias in attentional behavior. Furthermore, the companies selected for the interviews were members of different industries. Given these precautions, care was exercised when generalizing the interview findings to the entire population of MNEs.

In all, ten interviews were conducted with executives from nine different MNEs (Table 5-9). A third of these interviews were conducted in person. The majority of the interviews were conducted on the telephone because it was not possible to travel to each of the international destinations. All interviews were held with senior executives who were involved in the overall strategic direction of a company.

Table 5-9 **Respondents in Post-Test Interviews**

	Head-Office	Respondents
Accenture	Massachusetts (USA)	• Director, Institute for Strategic Change
Ansbacher Caribbean	Cayman Islands	• Regional Managing Director
Aurora Energy	Tasmania (Australia)	• General Manager, Retail
Dofasco	Ontario (CA)	• Director, Leadership Development
Fujitsu	New Jersey (USA)	• Executive VP, Organizational Capabilities • Senior VP, Leadership and Development
ICI	London (UK)	• Chief Information Officer
Medtronics	Minnesota (USA)	• Director, Executive & Leadership Development
Pinnacle Technologies	Dubai	• CEO and President
Wells Fargo	California (USA)	• EVP, Commercial Banking

The average time for each interview was approximately an hour. During this time, prepared, open-ended questions were asked about each MNE's practices, according to variables that were previously identified as being relevant. A summary of the post-test findings is provided below.

Behaviors normally associated with a global mindset

To further ensure face validity in this study, the interviews were started by asking respondents to identify behaviors that they would normally associate with globally minded managers. The views of MNE executives converged on factors that were included in this study: for example, using scanning activities to understand what's happening globally, communicating/building relationships with important stakeholders worldwide, and including international issues in executive committee meetings. In discussing the reasons that motivate these behaviors, several respondents indicated that managers with a global mindset possess a strong sense of curiosity. These managers understand the necessity of paying careful attention to international issues, for it is the only way to ensure that their assumptions are correct. Realizing that no universal approach to international business problems exists, globally minded managers were described to be low on the assumptive, and high on the analytic.

Tom Davenport – Director of the *Institute of Strategic Change* at Accenture, and a notable contributor to the field of attention research (Davenport and Beck, 2001) – provided a list of behaviors that globally-minded managers typically demonstrate:

> They realize that being global involves not just having global components within their organization, but spending a good deal of their mental capacity on international issues. They don't make hard and fast judgments about the way the world works. They view things as being more geographically dependent so they literally spend time in other parts of the world. They travel a lot, roughly once a month or so, and certainly would have telephone conversations with people all around the world. They read about other parts of the world a lot, and they are aware of markets and competitors in other parts of the world. They spread their attention more broadly from a geographical standpoint than managers who do not have global mindsets.

Dave Santi, Director of Leadership Development at Dofasco, offered interesting comments that help make more precise the relationship that exists between mindset and attention behaviors. Santi used the example of John Mayberry, his former boss at Dofasco, to illustrate his thoughts. Mayberry was getting ready for an important meeting with the company's board of directors, which had always given him a fair bit of resistance in the past. A picture of the world was situated in the corner of the room. This image of a globe initiated an interesting discussion with the board. Dave Santi recalls the nature of this conversation:

> Board: Why have you got that globe here? You're a small little steel company in North America, you're likely not going to be dealing on a global basis, you're not big enough!
> Mayberry: You're right and we'll still probably be focusing principally on our domestic market, but the interesting part is the rest of the world will be influencing how we will be doing business. We need to have a mindset in the organization, from top to bottom, that there are things that we'd better start thinking about. We may not be able to control them, but they are going to impact our business, like imports into Canada, consolidation, and over-supply of steel.

What this conversation suggests is that a global mindset truly resides, as its name indicates, in the mind of managers – what they think about throughout the course of their day-to-day activities. Behaviors are subsequently both a consequence of this mindset (people pay attention to things that are consistent with their frames of reference), and a determinant of it (mindsets evolve over time to integrate the results of past attentional efforts). Santi comments on this condition:

> I don't know if I would associate global mindsets with the word traveling – that happened to be an outcome or an enabler. John simply had the thinking that was much more global, and not narrow-minded. He understood there were other things throughout the world that really mattered to us. He drew the causal relationship between operating a small steel mill in Hamilton and the connection to what he had to change to ensure that Dofasco

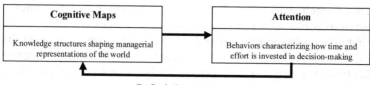

Figure 5-6   Components of a Global Mindset

remained profitable based on a whole bunch of environmental things that were happening on a global basis. He knew that there were steel mills around the world that were quite capable of landing in his backyard and firing up in two or three years.

Note that this conceptualization is consistent with the one presented in Chapter 1, where reciprocal links were formulated between mindset (a cognitive orientation) and attention (the behaviors that both result and determine the content of this orientation). It is useful to visualize this relationship in Figure 5-6, while also remembering that this research used an attention-based approach to the concept of global mindsets, emphasizing behaviors rather than cognitive maps or orientations to approximate this construct.

The social structure of attention

Consistent with Hypothesis 1, all respondents, without exception, agreed with the view that systems and structures have the potential to impact behaviors, especially as they relate to the formation of global mindsets. For example, Brad Neary, the Director, Executive & Leadership Development at Medtronic, elaborated on the role of incentives:

> To develop global mindsets, it is crucial to layout the game plan. Companies need to be clear on the competencies and behaviors they expect from their managers, and ensure that those who excel are rewarded with promotions. Companies must also take action against those who don't live within the guidelines. Public hangings can be very effective.

MNE top executives differed in other respects. Their responses, some of which are presented below, capture a diverse range of ideas that are quite characteristic of the complexity associated with the constructs they represent.

Structural positions. This study's finding that the use of structural positions would have a marginal impact on international attention did not surprise MNE top executives very much. The problem with globalization champions was often tied to credibility issues. Unless a CEO acts as a champion, globalization stories are typically not heard by top team members. Respondents recognized the importance of job titles and responsibilities for defining what people are and where they fit in an organization, but they often remained skeptical of their relevance to the concept of global mindsets. Addressing this situation, Neary observes:

> Using the word "global" in people's job titles is a little bit like putting the word "effective" in somebody's title, or talking about ebusiness as something very specific. It's just part of business. There is nothing special about it. Five or ten years ago, it was very important to talk about developing global leaders. Right now, a global leader is not a special person anymore, but a leader who happens to do his or her job in a global organization.

A few of the respondents, however, argued that structural positions nevertheless remain important mechanisms to consider. For one, structural positions act as reminders to managers that global mindsets are essential to their mandates, and these positions are perhaps critical at earlier stages of career and international expansion. Job titles also contain basic pieces of information that might be useful to outsiders. The title of a person is one of the few things that one sees on a business card, so it can quite effectively communicate the global interests and perspectives of specific managers. The following passages illustrate these viewpoints:

- Elliot Nelson, Senior Vice President Leadership at Fujitsu.

  Some people aren't impressed or moved by global job titles, but I think that they help establish a role and an understanding that you're not just thinking about one particular market, and you're not too narrow in your focus.

- Dave Santi, Director of Leadership Development at Dofasco.

I would agree that title may not determine capability, but I would think that it would have some influence on what you should be focusing on, and everything else should line up to that. I think title does dictate and has some influence on individual behavior. When Don went from being COO to CEO he started acting like the CEO and if he went to Chairman he'd start acting like the Chairman. So I think you can get something out of a title. However, it has to be supported by responsibilities and accountabilities in that job and what you're expecting in terms of outcomes.

Company resources. Respondents often indicated that top team members lack the resources that would help them develop a global perspective on things. According to Anthony Foster, Chief Information Officer at ICI, the problem resides in the fact that information technology gets used quite differently around the world, so that it can be quite difficult to get plugged to the right sources of information and people. Nevertheless, respondents agreed that the implementation of common systems and user-friendly platforms of communication would make it much easier for top team members to understand what is going on in various parts of the world. Respondents also cited other examples of company resources that they considered essential, such as the amount budgeted for travel, and the support given to executives as they prepare and return from their international assignments. For the majority of the interviewees, much progress remains to be made in terms of providing logistics that support the global mindset imperative.

Incentives. Only one respondent mentioned that he had never heard of "a conscious manipulation of incentives with an eye towards influencing what people attend to." But this individual immediately added: "but certainly there must be a strong influence." In the vast majority of cases, the interview findings emphasized the crucial role of incentives in shaping global mindsets. Interestingly, only three respondents mentioned rewards that involved actual financial components (e.g. shares, cash, or actual compensation bonuses tied to international growth objectives). Instead, the majority of executives believed in the power of long-term career advancement, and public pats on the back. For example, many companies appear to promote people when they achieve outstanding global results or when they make dedicated efforts to better comprehend the complexity of international business. Other companies give formal leadership awards to those individuals who have worked across businesses, cultures, or functions, and to those who have led a very broad scale global effort that has implications for the entire company. Congratulatory notes from the CEO were said to be another powerful device.

At the highest levels of the organization, respondents shared the view that career, ambition, learning objectives, commitment to the company, and the desire to win – or re-affirm a place in the company, or even in some cases, the industry – are the key factors that drive behaviors. Pure economic motives tend to be less important in explaining the formation of global mindsets at the executive level. As Martin Newton, Executive Vice President of Commercial Banking at Wells Fargo, indicates:

> When you think of things that motivate people, financial compensation is actually less important than a lot of other factors. Public recognition is more important – particularly for senior people – than money. The most important incentive to me would be a hand written note from the chairman saying that he personally noticed something that I did. This is more meaningful for my career path … it would tell me that the top people are watching me personally. In the end, everyone gets an increase in pay but not everyone gets recognized.

Interestingly, three respondents also mentioned symbolic incentives that were associated with a type of action learning. The following quote illustrates this idea, which may also provide a possible explanation for the high positive correlation (0.61) that was observed between symbolic incentives and leadership development variables (see Chapter 4). Peter Davis, General Manager of Aurora Retail, observes:

> Two of the companies I worked with – ABB and HP – had incentives around leadership development activities. They were viewed as a huge reward … for a very small number of senior managers around the world. They were international consortium programs … where

they selected their top people. There were programs run in Australia, US, Europe, etc. Participants aspired to be on these programs and everyone saw them participating.

Leadership development. Every single executive interviewed was able to think of several examples of leadership development activities that may have an impact on the development of global mindsets. In particular, several respondents emphasized the importance of international assignments and other forms of relocation initiatives. Providing managers with prolonged forms of global exposure, these mechanisms were understood to have a huge impact on the perspectives of managers, and on their motivation to pay careful attention to international issues. In addition, investments in education and training programs were identified as critical factors to consider.

The interview findings revealed, however, that such experiential programs turn out to be extremely costly for MNEs. Consistent with ideas already developed in international strategic management literature (e.g. Black et al., 1999a), the most talented executives happen to fail when placed in contexts that are different from their own, and too often leave a company upon their return. As a result, indications suggest that MNEs have been trying to achieve greater cultural sensitivity without such long-term, more expensive types of commitments. An increasingly popular solution today consists of asking people to work in multi-cultural teams for a certain period of time. The costs are limited since most of the team meetings are conducted through video-conference and collaboration software.

Another example involves the Canadian steel company Dofasco, which has innovated by creating entire communities of practice around the idea of globalization. Every year, it sends half-a-dozen managers to foreign customer plants in every part of the world so that they can better understand the changes that are affecting the business. It also delegates more participants to committee meetings of the *International Steel Association* than any other steel company in the world. Through this type of action learning, Dofasco is able to shape global mindsets without moving people around, without spending billions of dollars on their education, and without investing in foreign assignments.

The role of the MNE's environment of decisions

Interview data on the role of strategy and industry considerations was generally consistent with Hypothesis 2 for explaining the structuring of organizational practices. Nevertheless, three of the respondents called attention to the fact that a lot of inertia is embedded into MNEs. Often, the structures used by a firm to channel attention towards certain issues and away from others are described as obsolete, and are often tied to past strategic objectives. The following quote from Elliot Nelson, Senior Vice President at Leadership and Development at Fujitsu, illustrates the difficulty of keeping the content of attention structures attuned to strategic objectives that are rapidly changing:

> What drives the disconnect is the complexity in the market. The competitive pressure is coming to bear now because companies aren't making any money. So they are changing strategy like they change their underwear. It's almost daily ... . As a result, executives are always playing catch-up. The business model they started ten years ago no longer works so they're searching for something else.

Another source of inertia lies with top executives themselves, who may still be quite ethnocentric in their outlooks, and thus, unwilling to facilitate the adoption of international attention structures. This problem – which was evoked in terms of a "self-fulfilling prophecy" by Mike Hodgson, the Regional Managing Director for Ansbacher Caribbean – was often cited as a major obstacle to the development of global mindsets in MNEs. Similarly, Ron McCulloch, Executive VP Organizational Capabilities at Fujitsu, concludes:

> Most organizations are aggregations of national or international pieces of business run by groups of people that have a knowledge base of cultural experiences relatively narrow, biased towards where they have grown up and who they are. And if it's American then it's really narrow, and if it's European then it's much broader.

This source of inertia might also provide an explanation for the imperfect relationship observed between signals of an MNE's environment of decisions – global strategic posture, international interdependence, and international competition – and the extent to which top team members demonstrate global mindset behaviors (Hypothesis 3). In particular, several respondents noted that the type of structural positions, resources, incentives, and leadership development activities discussed in this study would not be implemented within an MNE, unless someone within the top team (usually the CEO) recognized the potential associated with the development of global mindsets.

For example, Ron McCulloch, the Executive Vice President of Organizational Capabilities at Fujitsu, referred this argument to explain corporate decisions to bring "a non-conformer" within a top team. In the end, the disruptive effect generated by the introduction of a new player (for example, Carlos Gohn in the case of the Renault-Nissan alliance) may constitute an effective way to "challenge the thinking in process" (i.e. modify the social structure of attention), and force the formation of global mindsets within a top team.

Performance implications of global mindset behaviors

The reactions of top executives to this study's finding that a global mindset constitutes a mixed blessing in terms of financial performance differed. Approximately a third of the respondents indicated surprise. In their minds, thinking about international issues makes sense, regardless of the costs involved. The rest of the respondents indicated strong qualitative support to this study's performance finding. The reasons offered justifying the nature of the relationship between international attention and overall company performance include (1) loss of focus, (2) excessive interference from headquarters, and (3) over-simplification problems. The following passages illustrate each of these issues in turn.

Loss of focus.

- Mike Hodgson, Ansbacher Caribbean

  I would say it's not very surprising that business is suffering. It's cumbersome to manage a business globally. The toughest thing I find in being a general manager is balancing the time between

internal stuff, chasing new clients throughout the world, representing the company at various events, a bit of philanthropic
activity, staff demands, communication issues .... Balancing all
those constituencies is hard. But if global executives allow any of
those demands to push the others to the side, they are not doing
a good job in terms of maintaining company performance.

- Dave Santi, Director of Leadership Development at Dofasco

Having a global mind-mindset can be very confusing. It's a big
problem. Bill Chisholm used to be responsible for our Mexican
operations. His time in Mexico was three weeks out of a month,
and only one week on the road. Then all of a sudden, we bought
two plants and we gave him two plants up here in Hamilton.
Now he's a week in Mexico, a week in Ohio, a week in Hamilton,
and the a week somewhere else. He's trying to deal with all of
these things simultaneously, but he feels he's lost a little sense of
the operational issues on a week-to-week, or day-to-day basis.

Excessive interference from corporate headquarters.

- Tom Davenport, Director, Institute of Strategic Change Accenture

I guess we could also speculate that there is too much micro-
management going on. Up to a point, it would be useful for the
company if global executives devoted some of their attention
to operations in other parts of the world. Beyond that point,
they would be meddling in things they shouldn't be meddling
instead of giving people who run those operations a little bit
more autonomy.

Over-simplification.

- Anthony Foster, Chief Information Officer at ICI

A global mindset is nice to have but it's also confusing. I would
say the old saying, the devil's in the details, and if you're not
careful you may generalize too much and get yourself in trouble.
So yes, I think your inverted "U" makes a lot of sense. I also think

in terms of layers. I've got a global business; I've got local managers pounding away in local markets; and I may have another layer of regional managers on top of that. By paying too much attention to international issues, executives at the corporate headquarters may be trying to optimize layers that are simply concerned with local market conditions and not at all preoccupied with the bigger picture.

6
Interpretation and Extensions

In this chapter, the results are interpreted in light of their implications for research on the topic of attention, as well as for theories of global mindsets in MNEs. Much of the argument is designed to extend this research's results to broader issues of multinational management, and thus, it is quite prescriptive in nature. As such, the discussion provided in this chapter may be of interest to both academic researchers and practitioners. The chapter is divided into four sections. The first section provides a brief summary interpretation of the research findings in light of past and existing research dealing with the topic of global mindsets. From this discussion, three themes emerged that are the subject of further discussion: (1) the MNE as a matrix of inter-connected minds, (2) global mindsets and the concept of geographic competency, and (3) the viability of a number of alternate globalization strategies for MNEs. These themes will be addressed in the second, third, and fourth sections of the chapter.

6.1 Summary interpretation of the research findings

Three overarching research questions were addressed in the research. (1) What does the concept of a global mindset mean for MNEs? (2) What are the different approaches used by MNEs to foster the development of global mindsets among their top management teams? And which ones are the most effective? (3) And what are the performance implications of global mindsets? These questions were investigated in a three-year, multi-phased research project. Eighteen in-depth field interviews were used as preliminary observations of the research objectives. Building on attention theory, a conceptual framework was proposed to map the relationships that were relevant to the research objectives previously identified. A sample of 900 medium and large MNEs in 13 industries and 6 countries (United States, Canada, Japan, France, Germany, and the United Kingdom) was then assembled as the basis for data collection.

The validity of the conceptual framework was subsequently assessed using three different data sources: questionnaire data from 136 MNEs that was analyzed using principal component analysis, cluster analysis, and multivariate regression techniques; secondary data that was obtained for key controls and performance measures; and finally, post-hoc interviews that involved ten top executives from nine different MNEs.

What the concept of a global mindset means for MNEs

The first research objective of this research was to clarify the domain of the global mindset construct. A basic definition of global mindset implies the notion of executives who can get their minds around the whole world, not just a few "lead markets." It implies the capacity to pay attention to all important issues, events and trends, regardless of where they happen in the world. A critical point that is often emphasized in international strategic management literature is that the acquisition of a global mindset requires individual managers to have a core set of global leadership skills (Black et al., 1999b; Adler & Bartholomew, 1992). For example, globally competent managers are often described as being more aware and tolerant of cultural norms and interpersonal differences. In most cases, this greater cultural sensitivity or readiness to see the world as their oyster can be understood as the result of repeated efforts on the part of top team members to expose themselves to the inherent complexity of international business.

Building on this over-arching assumption, this research identified behaviors that are normally associated with a global mindset. Three categories of factors were subsequently discussed.

- Collecting and analyzing information pertaining to global business developments.

- Communicating and building relationships with important constituencies worldwide (overseas managers, key customers, suppliers, etc.).
- Using executive committee meetings to integrate relevant international issues into a company's decision-making process.

The descriptive statistics presented in Appendix C indicate that top executives in MNEs make a significant use of the behaviors that are associated with a global mindset. For example, in this study, the time spent by a CEO traveling around the world for business purposes averaged 25 percent with a standard deviation of 16, and a range of 0 to 80 percent. This information indicates that 95 percent of the CEOs in the set of responding companies spend between 9 and 41 percent of their time outside their home countries. The qualitative data also reveals that MNE top executives use the other categories of behaviors to a significant degree. It is also interesting to remember that important differences were noted across industries, countries, and different types of organizational contexts. For example, French or British top executives spend approximately 30 percent more time and effort scanning the world's environment compared to those operating North American companies (see Table C2).

Nevertheless, virtually all the executives interviewed during the course of this research project emphasized that MNEs are often seriously lacking in managers who have a strong global mindset. According to the evidence provided in Chapter 3, ethnocentric thinking is still prevalent in most top management groups, even in those companies that pursue the most global strategies.

Perhaps an easier way to illustrate this problem is with an anecdote that came to the mind of one of the executives interviewed during the course of this research. This respondent was convinced that one of his direct colleagues (a senior Vice President in the company) had been giving serious thoughts to the Japanese market as evidenced by his frequent trips to Japan. But the research revealed that while this individual traveled to Japan every eight weeks, he watched US movies on the airplane trip, stayed at a US hotel chain in Tokyo, and experienced few interactions with local customers or suppliers. His typical day in Tokyo consisted of an 8:30am trip from the hotel to the company's local office, meetings with American expatriate managers, some office work which included frequent phone calls back to the US and work on home-office email, and then a return trip to the hotel at about 5:30pm. How much attention did he give to important Japanese issues?

As this anecdote suggests, even the most senior executives in MNEs can see foreign markets through an essentially domestic filter. Clearly, it is not easy to keep track of what is going on in the minds of executives over extended periods of time. Nevertheless, a close examination of their day-to-day behaviors offers clues about the things that capture their attention, and thus, a good indication of the extent to which they have developed strong global mindsets.

Approaches used by MNEs to foster global mindsets in top managers

Based on evidence that companies are eager to increase the number of executives with global mindsets (Govindarajan & Gupta, 2001; Doz et al., 2001), this research's second research objective was to determine the most effective approaches used by companies to develop global mindsets. Consistent with attention theory, it was found that the *structures* that firms create to channel the limited attention of managers towards certain activities and away from others are the strongest predictors of global mindsets. Specifically, four categories of attention structures were identified:

- Structural positions
- Company resources
- Incentives
- Leadership development

Structural positions define the roles, identities, and obligations of top managers in an organization. In particular, global job titles and re-sponsibilities, as well as the influence of globalization champions, can be used to shape the behaviors of top managers, and to ensure that they see the acquisition and maintenance of a global mindset as a duty that constitutes an important part of their job requirements.

Company resources are the tangible and intangible assets that are utilized by a top team to accomplish critical MNE tasks. Resources such as the IT infrastructure – which should be designed to allow quick and easy access to relevant information sources across the entire company – are critical for supporting behaviors that one would normally associate with a global mindset.

Incentives are also important to consider. In general, managers appear to be more likely to demonstrate behaviors characteristic of global mindsets if they are given material rewards, social status, and credits in the process. Incentives of a symbolic nature (e.g. career prospects, public recognition, etc.) are particularly meaningful to managers, for they often reflect an MNE's true identity or purpose.

Finally, leadership development activities play a central role in the development of global mindsets. Training programs, international assignments, teamwork, job rotations across countries, and mentoring initiatives are powerful tools for shaping the global perspectives of top managers, and thus, influencing their behaviors. Each of these activities provides top team members with an opportunity to learn about the various countries, cultures, and customers that make up the world's marketplace, thereby facilitating the emergence of global mindset behaviors.

Relative effectiveness of the various approaches

A recent Forum in *Harvard Business Review* (Green et al., 2003) asked five of the world's top executives (four CEOs and the head of an international recruiting company) to describe their company experience with globalization. To a large extent, their responses echo some of the ideas discussed in this research. All agree, for example, that one of the most important criteria for MNE success is to have leaders who are free of strong geographic biases. Interestingly, however, the executives participating in this forum differed on issues pertaining to the development of global mindsets. The following discussion captures ideas that are related to the concepts of structural positions, company incentives, and leadership development activities.

Michael Marks, CEO of Flextronics, argues that "the most capable executives" he has known have "gained their broad perspectives in the course of their work." In his view, structural positions (e.g. job titles and responsibilities) create obligations and patterns of social interactions that are essential for cultivating global mindsets within a top team. Among other things, Marks observes:

> Flextronics's top management team orchestrates manufacturing activity in 28 different countries and leads sales operations

worldwide. The peer group includes a CFO from New Zealand, a CTO from Grenada, a sales executive from Ireland, and business unity heads from Sweden, Great Britain, India, Singapore, and Hong Kong. It's hard to work in such an environment and remain provincial in your outlook.

Fred Hassan, Chairman and CEO of Schering-Plough, believes in the value of economic incentives, including behavior-based performance evaluation systems. Reflecting upon the initiatives that his company adopted in order to promote global attitudes in their managers and to diminish their tendency towards stereotyping, Hassan reveals:

> We went through a big change process to end that kind of thinking. We established new performance expectations that measured how well our employees demonstrated open-minded behaviors, including shared accountability, transparency, and collaboration across geographies.

Stephen Green, Group CEO HSBC, also believes in the importance of incentives, but ones centered on career prospects and the acquisition of international experience rather than systems of performance evaluation. He argues:

> No one gets to the top at HSBC without having worked in more than one market. If you look at the executives currently running the company's largest businesses, all of them have worked in more than one, and nearly all in more than two, major country markets.

In contrast, Daniel Meiland, Executive Chairman at Egon Zehnder International emphasizes the limits of such mechanisms. The acquisition of global mindsets is a difficult process that does not simply follow from initiatives aimed at providing managers with greater international exposure. Meiland concludes:

> Many companies still believe the best way to help managers develop a global mindset is to put them in positions in other countries. But that hasn't been very effective, primarily because companies station people abroad and then forget about them... .

Also, many people have reasons for not wanting to hop from location to location. For one, it's easier to develop client relationships if you stay in one place for an extended period of time. Those client relationships can be very important when it comes to getting promoted.

Jeffrey Immelt, Chairman and CEO of General Electric, insists on the value of leadership development activities and adequate incentive systems:

> We spend $1 billion in training, which has the most important benefit of connecting people across the company. We also move people around a lot, for the same reason... A lot of people have said that GE could be more global by moving its headquarters overseas, for example by moving its medical systems business from Milwaukee to Paris... but ... it's truly about people, not about where the buildings are. You've got to develop people so that they are prepared for leadership jobs, and then promote them. That's the most effective way to become more global.

This research provides a great opportunity to put this dialogue into perspective by testing the relative effectiveness of the various approaches used by MNEs to cultivate global mindsets in key managers. Hierarchical analysis was used to separate the effects associated with structural positions, company resources, economic and symbolic incentives, and leadership development activities (Table 5-1). Taken in isolation, each category of attention structure exerts some impact on the behaviors of managers, contributing unique variances in international attention. As a result, the structures identified in this research are all worth considering by MNEs.

Nevertheless, attention structures are not equally effective. Structural positions, resources, and economic incentives explained much less variance in the dependent variable than did categories such as leadership development and symbolic incentives. In addition, when all attention structures were included in the same regression model, the role of structural positions dropped significantly in importance. The variables labeled symbolic incentives and leadership development were the only ones to remain significant at $p < 0.01$ when all five structures were considered simultaneously.

Therefore, the results reported in this research emphasize where companies should begin to focus their efforts when considering the global mindset imperative. Their emphasis should be first on developing a culture and a purpose that associates symbolic rewards with the pursuit of global mindset behaviors. Next, their emphasis should be on leadership development activities, including training programs, international assignments, cross-border business teams, job rotations across countries, and mentoring initiatives. All these mechanisms can help managers become more aware of cultural norms and interpersonal differences, while also helping them to forge critical international relationships.

In the final analysis, MNEs also need to be aware of the costs involved when deciding which initiatives are worth pursuing in order to motivate the acquisition of global mindsets. For example, while global job titles and responsibilities exert a limited impact on the behaviors, and more particularly, the degree of attention that managers invest in international issues, the use of such structural positions is quite inexpensive, compared to the $1 billion that GE spends every year on training initiatives. Therefore, these options should not be discarded. The field interviews also yielded insights on this cost-benefit trade-off. If international assignments and job rotations across countries were often presented as being powerful mechanisms of global exposure, the respondents often stressed limitations as well. In particular, these options appear to be of limited value unless an MNE takes special care to facilitate departure, track people over time, and ensure that they are not forgotten when they come back. Clearly, the most effective tools to develop global mindsets are also the most expensive ones.

Other important drivers of a global mindset

The attention-focusing role of other key variables was also examined. In particular, the impact of an MNE's environment of decisions was investigated along three key dimensions: (1) the expansiveness of an MNE's global strategic posture, which refers to the extent to which a company depends on foreign sales and foreign-placed resources (assets and employees); (2) the international interdependence of an MNE's operations, i.e. the degree to which an MNE's value-added activities are coordinated across worldwide locations; and (3) the amount of international competition prevailing within an MNE's industry. The results indicate a positive relationship between these three variables and behaviors characteristic of a global mindset. However, this relationship is also imperfect, and partially dependent upon a company's attention structures. Specifically, the results indicate that global strategic posture, international interdependence, and international competition impact what types of structural positions, company resources, leadership development, and incentive systems are selected by an organization. This configuration of attention structures that results, in turn, explains how top managers spend some of their time and mental energy. In other words, the international content of an MNE's attention structures was found to partially mediate the relationship between an MNE's environment of decisions and international attention.

Top team characteristics were found to have only a limited influence on the construct of international attention. While cultural heterogeneity (nationality-based) has a significant impact on the time and efforts that a company's top executives spend thinking about international issues, the influence of accumulated international experience is not statistically significant. In addition, the effect that international experience exerts on the choice of attention structure loses its statistical significance when indicators of international activity (e.g. global strategic posture, international interdependence, and international competition) are taken into account. These results are worth discussing in that they provide a counterpoint to widely-shared views established in international strategic management literature.

From a theoretical standpoint, the limited role of international experience is consistent with social theory perspectives, and Ocasio's (1997: 189) principle of situated attention, "in which the cognition and action of individuals are not predictable from the knowledge of individual characteristics but are derived from the specific organizational context and situations that individual decision-makers mind themselves in." Therefore, while international experience likely determines the skills and tacit knowledge acquired by the top team, it only has a marginal impact on the day-to-day behaviors of managers and the choice of attention structures. It is also possible to speculate that while international experience makes managers more receptive to the global thinking imperative, at some point, it also diminishes the importance of paying careful attention to international issues.

Managers who have accumulated substantial experience in overseas assignments are likely to have developed skills that allow them to achieve a greater understanding of worldwide business conditions without investing a lot of attention in the process. In other words, the concept of a global mindset may have become so engrained in managers' competency profiles that it requires less investment of time and effort. As a result, MNEs should seek initiatives aimed at shaping the international experience of managers. Methodological caveats are also discussed in the final chapter of this research that addresses the limitations of the research.

Performance implications of a global mindset

A curvilinear relationship was found between international attention and MNE performance. Several things are worth highlighting in the light of this finding. First, the observed variance in company success emphasizes the inevitable scarcity of resources in most companies and the inability of managers to attend to every possible strategic issue (Morrison, Bouquet, & Beck, 2004). In other words, the allocation of attention entails a zero-sum game (Gifford, 1992; Hansen & Haas, 2001). That is, time spent traveling internationally or discussing with managers overseas is not available for other issues important to the organization. Not only are the costs of international attention associated with missed opportunities but they can also reflect real, out-of-pocket expenses for companies. For example, General Electric spends an average of $1 billion every year training its executives to become more receptive to the complexity of the world in which they operate (Green et al., 2003).

This does not mean to suggest, however, that global mindsets do not matter at all. Certainly MNEs need to monitor and comprehend issues on a true worldwide basis. What our results question is not the general value of internationalizing management's attention, but rather the importance of this objective to a company's top executives as opposed to middle or junior managers. Essentially, our findings demonstrate that too much global environmental surveillance at the very top executive levels may ultimately be detrimental to firm performance. And therein lies an interesting paradox. On one hand, leaders in the twenty-first century have to become aware of all critical developments worldwide. On the other hand, their ability to attend to the entire range of all important issues is limited. Perhaps the key to effective global leadership lies in how well MNE top executives manage and mobilize the attention of *subordinates* at the corporate center or in foreign locations, to achieve global mindsets without excessive attention on their part.

Moreover, the attention-performance picture observed in this study only constitutes a snapshot in time that tells us little about future performance outcomes. Like any type of investment, the allocation of scarce attention by top executives is expensive, but the rewards can also be substantial. Among other things, future benefits can result from greater abilities to innovate, or strengthen ties with distant customers. While investing time and effort on international issues can possibly have a disruptive short-term effect on pure profitability figures, it may very well enhance the long-term prospects of a company. Company initiatives that reflect this preoccupation with the long-term potential of allocating attention to international issues were also identified during the course of the field interviews. For example, two of the interviewed companies have created dedicated units to watch worldwide trends and developments, and/or markets that may be still too marginal to deserve the scarce attention of a company's top executives, yet promising of significant future rewards. The corporate entrepreneurship literature, specifically as it relates to the role of incubators and other bottom-up processes used to champion innovative ideas (Burgelman, 1983b; Day, 1994), is useful to understand the value of such international units. Jean-Yves Leblanc, Chairman of Bombardier Transportation also comments on the function of Bombardier International, and how it helps to preserve the scarce attention of busy MNE managers while enhancing the long-term learning abilities of the company.

> For a number of years, we had been thinking that we needed to pay some attention to Russia. An idea was to start with Aerospace and acquire some subcontractors over there. But six months later, we would be in a meeting to find out it had remained a very low-priority for the operating groups because they had so much to do already. As we did not want to miss the opportunity, we ask ourselves: "How can we get organized?" And then we got the idea of having Bombardier International.
>
> The mission and role of Bombardier International is to focus on markets that the operating groups have identified but for

which they don't have the time and resources to devote right away. For two or three years, they go gather the data and at the same time they do develop the network and company presence. Then they come back with a very good, solid market analysis that advises us on what to do in specific markets, and on how to do it.

Another point worth emphasizing with respect to the attention-performance relationship is that the analysis was principally conducted using hard accounting figures. When other soft components of firm success were taken into account (e.g. employee development, the perceived reputation of the MNE in the industry, and the quality of its products and services), international attention was found to actually have a positive and linear relationship with performance. Again, the cultivation of a global mindset may thus represent a valid goal, even if it yields mixed implications in terms of immediate pure profitability figures. As Daniel Meiland, Executive Chairman of Egon Zehnder International (Green et al., 2003: 42) indicates, global mindsets are essential for ensuring the professional and personal development of managers:

> Developing a global mindset and learning about other cultures are important for your career, of course, but they are also enriching on a very personal level. We all need to experience other cultures and ideas to grow as individuals. And to some degree, that individual growth intertwines with the professional.

In light of this foundation, the determinants and performance implications of a global mindset can be better understood. This discussion is pursued through an examination of three distinct themes, which remain largely unexplored in international strategic management literature: (1) conceptualizing an MNE as a matrix of interconnected minds, (2) global mindset and the concept of geographic competency, and (3) viability of alternate globalization strategies. It is useful to remember that the remainder of this chapter goes beyond the research's immediate results. As noted earlier, many of the comments are prescriptive in nature; thus, they suggest a variety of implications that may be relevant to academic researchers, as well as to practicing managers.

6.2   Conceptualizing the MNE as a matrix of inter-connected minds

In 1965, Canadian media theorist Marshall McLuhan declared that rapid telecommunications advances and jet travel were about to create a global village where time would cease to exist and space vanish. Likewise, modern disciples of McLuhan such as Peter Drucker (1993; 1999), and Alvin and Heidi Toffler (1993) have repeatedly suggested that today's technological revolution has facilitated the emergence of an electronic society where people and information sources can quickly and easily connect to one another, regardless of the distance that separates them.

The basic precept of the global village metaphor is that the information age in which MNEs now operate is rapidly affecting the speed at which international transactions are conducted. Through media such as the telephone, video-conferencing, and more recently emails, in a matter of seconds MNE executives can potentially become aware of issues and events that take place thousands of miles away. Like if technology had almost become a biological extension of their senses.

However, by evoking the image of a global village, McLuhan (1965) was likely trying to convey the message that rapid technological advances were racing ahead of people's ability to make sense of the information that is (at least theoretically) available to them. Simply stated, the current proliferation of information represents a problematic development for rational people will only consider those pieces of information that first capture their attention, those that they believe are the most significant. Regardless of how much information is at their fingertips, executives will still make choices in terms of what issues are likely to be salient in their minds: what they worked on during their long hours at work, or what they obsessed over during the last executive committee meeting.

Based on this reasoning, the issue for MNEs is not simply to determine whether a plethora of information sources exist to support executive decisions. Rather, the critical issue is to ensure that the right pieces of information receive the careful attention of executives. The results of this research indicate that companies are well advised to integrate sound principles of attention management to assist in this task. To start with, they should ensure that structural

positions, company resources, incentives, and leadership development activities are deployed in ways that support the organization's
key objectives. Only through such a carefully orchestrated effort can
an organization ensure that the day-to-day actions of all executives
remain consistent with the strategic and industry context.

The possibilities of attention management are endless. In a recent
article of *Wired* (2003), journalist and author Steven Johnson evoked
the dream of a society organized around the notion of "mind-
share." It describes a civilization where people are connected not
around a set of documents and fountains of information sources,
but around "what is going on in another person's head over
extended periods." This civilization is based on the assumption that
people freely maintain personal back-logs of every significant event
or information item that they find particularly relevant, i.e. things
that capture their most precious attention. These postmodern forms
of diaries would themselves be linked to one another in a sort of
giant matrix that would be accessible to all. Johnson encourages
readers to imagine this civilization where people could access documents based on trust factors: "this particular information item is
useful because six minds I admire have paid attention to it."

The next generation of knowledge management systems in MNEs
could integrate this matrix of connected minds into their principles
of functioning. Rather than indexing documents and best practices
in terms of key words (e.g. topics), these systems would also indicate
the accumulated attention received by each item stored in the database. Of course, such a system would not be designed to generate
a list of "most-popular items" in the database. Instead, it would
allow managers to identify events and ideas that a colleague known
for his/her particular expertise on a given topic has found most
significant. This system would preserve the scarce attention and
time of managers, while also making the search for intelligence and
wisdom more promising.

6.3   Global mindset and the concept of geographic competency

International strategic management research has been largely preoccupied with the concept of firm-level competencies. For example,
Vernon (1966), Hymer (1976), and Dunning (1974) identify the

basic rationale for international diversification in ways that stress the importance of a company's most valuable assets, qualities such as a unique technological skill, a strong brand name, or any other input that differentiates an MNE from its competitors. Broadly defined, competencies refer to all sets of organizational factors that managers believe to be a source of competitive advantage.

Typically, researchers define competencies around products and services, which are assumed to be core when they define a company's fundamental business (Teece, Pisano, & Shuen, 1997: 516). As such, one of Eastman Kodak's core competencies might involve digital imaging. In contrast, display systems might be among Casio's core competencies, while sticky tape might be one of 3M's core competencies. According to strategy researchers, companies should make every effort to identify which products and services truly support their competitive advantage in order to enhance core competencies through investments in needed resources, and to develop a corporate wide infrastructure that encourages a core competency mindset at all levels of the organization (Prahalad & Hamel, 1991).

Embracing core competencies means that managers examine all possible decisions of product and market diversification in light of a company's proprietary skills and assets. According to Prahalad and Hamel (1991: 87), managers need to ask the following essential questions: "Does the new market opportunity add to the overall goal of becoming the best player in the world? Does it exploit or add to the core competence?" Companies that carefully assess these questions are expected to be the most effective at transferring their core competencies to other product and geographic markets, and should thus be in a position to make the most of their diversification strategies. As such, the process of transferring core competencies constitutes an essential quality of the "ownership" advantage that Dunning describes in his eclectic framework of multinational activity (1988).

Nevertheless, substantial evidence suggests that several barriers limit the transfer of core competencies within an MNE (Kostova, 1999). Some of these barriers are related to the characteristics of the practices being transferred for core competencies are often sticky, or they may not be always separable from the specific organizational and cultural context in which they are embedded (Ghoshal &

Bartlett, 1988; Szulanski, 1996; Zander & Kogut, 1995). On many occasions, headquarters' requests for implementation of a particular practice may also face resistance from foreign subsidiary managers. Birkinshaw and Fry (1998) specifically describe the corporate immune system that tends to fight the advancement of ideas and practices that come from outside a given geographical neighborhood. Aside from these barriers, an MNE must initially surmount the liability of foreignness often ascribed to its practices that lack legitimacy when implemented abroad (Zaheer, 1995), and it must acquire essential foreign market knowledge about how to operate effectively in otherwise unfamiliar cultures and environments (Johanson & Vahlne, 1977).

These requirements suggest that *geographic competencies* are key to understanding MNE success. Unlike core competencies, which are centered on products and markets (e.g. Sony's miniaturization skills), geographic competencies mean that a firm is competent to compete within a given country market. To paraphrase Prahalad and Hamel (1991: 81), an MNE is a large tree with limbs in multiple country locations, leaves across multiple product lines, and typically, flowers in multifunction activities, such as sales, manufacturing, human resources, etc. Binding these multiple dimensions in ways that preserve the coherence of the whole constitutes a significant challenge for MNEs (Doz & Prahalad, 1991).

Geographic competencies represent the glue that holds an MNE's portfolio of foreign country markets together. These competencies involve a deeper understanding of the similarities and differences that exist across local markets. In addition, they require the cultivation of valuable relationships with important constituencies worldwide (e.g. customers, suppliers, host-country public officials, universities, local trade associations, etc.), as well as the capacity to learn from ideas or practices that may well be created in remote and sometimes obscure locations. Geographic competencies are essential for competing effectively around the world, and for coordinating diverse operations across a set of geographically dispersed locations. They constitute the collective learning of an MNE's accumulated globalization efforts, and as such, often provide a guide for decisions related to issues of geographic diversification.

Like all skills and capabilities, geographic competencies will often deteriorate with time in the absence of appropriate investments. For example, the tacit knowledge that a company has acquired about how to operate effectively in Thailand may fade if no significant efforts are made to stay on top of relevant developments. As noted earlier in the discussion of the field interviews, the amount of attention that a company's top team gives to international strategic issues seems of paramount importance in understanding whether significant efforts are made to refresh an MNE's geographic competencies. By exhibiting a strong global mindset in their decision-making activities, executives help to ensure that their knowledge and understanding of the activities of an MNE portfolio remain current and updated to the realities of business.

Clearly, the results of this research indicate that by investing too much attention on foreign markets, MNE top executives may perhaps put excessive emphasis on developing the geographic competency of their company to the detriment of maintaining competencies in vital core products or services. This situation may arise when geographic competency becomes a core rigidity, bringing with it some important, and largely negative implications for firm performance (Leonard Barton, 1992).

6.4 Alternate globalization strategies for MNEs

International strategic management research has identified several options available to MNEs as they contemplate the process of international expansion. Alternate globalization strategies can be mapped using the *"global integration – local responsiveness (I – R) framework* developed by Prahalad and Doz (1987). According to this framework, MNEs choose a globalization strategy by continually balancing pressures for the global integration of activities and pressures for local responsiveness. Based on this framework, the strategies followed by an MNE can be of four types (Bartlett & Ghoshal, 1989). International strategies are based on transferring a company's knowledge through worldwide diffusion. Multidomestic strategies emphasize sensitivity to local market conditions. Global strategies focus on achieving efficiency through centralized globally integrated operations. Transnational strategies are designed to simultaneously achieve local responsiveness and efficiency advantages simultaneously, as articulated through such slogans as "think global, act local" that are characteristic of this approach. More recently, the model of a "meta-national corporation" has been proposed to foreground the importance of leveraging potentially valuable pockets of knowledge and expertise that are scattered around the world (Doz et al., 2001).

This stream of research provides the field of international strategic management with a rich theory of the MNE. This research offers an important extension to this dialogue by emphasizing the cognitive challenge of globalization. The activity/attention matrix, shown in Figure 6-1, reveals a systematic means for categorizing alternate strategies of internationalization (Morrison, Beck & Bouquet, 2004; Davenport & Beck, 2001). The matrix illustrates some of the possible variations in strategy associated with levels of international strategic activity in an MNE's environment of decisions, and the degree to which top team members focus their limited attention on international issues.

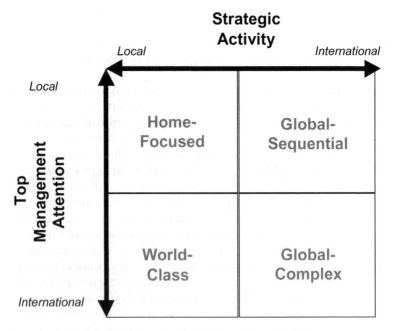

Figure 6-1   The Activity–Attention Matrix: Four Strategic Archetypes

Four strategic archetypes

Whether the MNEs represented in this sample can be mapped on this matrix represents the initial question that must be examined. The cluster analysis reported in Chapter 5 was used to classify MNEs according to indicators of international activity in the environment of decisions. Specifically, the scores obtained by each company on the global strategic posture, international interdependence, and international competition variables were used to partition the sample into two groups, representing low and high levels of international activity. A median split was used to create groupings of firms based on the international attention variable. Through these procedures, it was possible to determine the strategies pursued by MNEs, based on the activity-attention dimensions discussed above. Representative characteristics associated with each quadrant in the global activity-attention matrix are presented in Table 6-1.

- Thirty eight companies (28 percent of this sample) belonged to the *home-focused* quadrant, which includes companies that concentrate their activities in a few select locations, and that are heavily preoccupied by local market conditions.
- Thirteen companies (9.3 percent of the sample) were found to pursue a *world-class* strategy. While similar in many respects to companies in the first quadrant, world-class competitors actively search the world for new sources of ideas and worldwide learning opportunities. Their strategies are based on the internationalization of management attention, and the localization of key strategic activities.
- *Global sequential* strategies were followed by 33 MNEs (24 percent of the sample.) This third quadrant includes companies that have secured a commanding international presence, but whose top managers pay significantly less attention to ideas and events generated outside the home country. Operations are optimized on a country-by-country basis, with little interference from headquarters managers. Foreign affiliates are free to focus on meeting local customer needs.
- *Global complex* strategies involve high levels of strategic activity around the world and international attention. These complex forms of organizations, which have internationalized more of their activities and attention than companies in the other quadrants, represent the largest group of MNEs within this sample (n = 52, 38 percent of the sample).

Table 6-1   Characteristics of Archetype Types

	Home-Focused (n = 38)	World Class (n = 13)	Global Sequential (n = 33)	Global Complex (n = 52)
Age	47.3	37.7	64.3	61.7
Number of employees (thousands)	6.8	6.7	14.5	42.1
R&D intensity	4.8	8.9	4.8	10.8
Number of 2-digit SIC codes	2.5	2.2	2.3	2.6
Top team size	5.0	4.1	5.8	6.1
Number of nationalities within top team	1.8	2.5	2.3	3.6
Number of executives with international experience	0.7	0.9	1.8	2.5
Size of the board	9.6	9.3	10.1	11.3
Working capital (five year average)	0.3	0.4	0.2	0.3
Long term debt/common equity (five year average)	0.4	0.3	0.5	0.6
Activity Dimension				
Percentage of revenues that comes from international sales	35.00	50.5	56.0	63.2
Percentages of assets that comes from foreign locations	18.90	17.6	37.8	52.2
Percentage of employees that is based abroad	18.9	24.8	44.4	57.1
Number of countries in which the MNE operates	4.9	5.8	16.7	29.0
International interdependence (range of 9 to 36)	20.0	21.7	27.5	29.4
Amount of international competition in the industry (1–7 scale)	4.3	4.8	4.6	4.9

Table 6-1 Characteristics of Archetype Types – *continued*

Attention Dimension	Home-Focused (n = 38)	World Class (n = 13)	Global Sequential (n = 33)	Global Complex (n = 52)
Use of global scanning activities (1–7 scale)	3.6	4.8	3.0	4.6
Communications with overseas managers (range of 1 to 7)	4.3	5.3	4.4	5.5
Average time spent by the CEO traveling abroad (%)	13.4	25.8	20.9	35.4
Decision-making (1–7 scale)	3.3	4.3	3.7	5.1

Performance patterns

A follow-up question was needed in order to determine whether performance differences existed across companies in each of these four quadrants. Previous research on the topic argued that strategies associated with the four archetypes are all potentially viable (Davenport & Beck, 2001). In this context, MNEs are expected to rationally select the strategy that makes the most sense to them by continually balancing the potential for international activity simultaneously with their ability to focus attention internationally. An alternative view contends that companies with global activities should perform better when their top managers spread attention across geographic borders.

Descriptive statistics were used to analyze performance patterns in the global activity-attention matrix. First, the performance of activity and attention clusters was examined using five-year averages of return on assets, return on equity, return on investments, and return on sales (values are unstandardized, but adjusted for industry effects and risk). The results of this analysis are presented in Table 6-2, which reveals that the companies that are more internationally oriented tend to perform better, on average, than the less internationally oriented companies, although none of the differences are statistically significant at $p < 0.05$. Similarly, companies with higher levels of international attention and activities are associated with better performance levels, but the differences are so small that they are not statistically significant. The performance associated with each of the four strategic archetypes was also compared (Table 6-3.) Again, caution needs to be exercised in interpreting these data patterns, since none of the differences observed between groups are statistically significant at the 0.05 level.

Nevertheless, a couple of interesting insights are worth noting. First, world-class competitors appear to systematically out-perform companies that are more focused on local markets. By keeping international issues at the forefront, top management's attention may bring higher performance levels when companies operate in contexts characterized by limited international activity.

Second, global sequential competitors often achieve higher performance levels than global complex competitors. This relatively surprising finding suggests that high levels of international activity are sometimes more efficiently managed when top team members

Table 6-2 Performance Differences Across Activity-Attention Dimensions[a]

	5-Year ROA[b]	5-Year ROE[b]	5-Year ROI[b]	5-Year ROS[b]	Average
Activity Dimension					
• LOCAL	0.30	0.23	0.21	0.15	0.22
• GLOBAL	0.42	0.27	0.38	0.35	0.35
Attention Dimension					
• LOCAL	0.35	0.22	0.29	0.26	0.28
• GLOBAL	0.40	0.30	0.35	0.28	0.33

Table 6-3 Performance Differences Across Strategic Archetypes[a]

	5-Year ROA[b]	5-Year ROE[b]	5-Year ROI[b]	5-Year ROS[b]	Average
Strategic archetypes					
Home Focused	0.25	0.19	0.14	0.15	0.18
World Class	0.45	0.34	0.42	0.11	0.33
Global Sequential	0.47	0.25	0.47	0.39	0.39
Global Complex	0.39	0.29	0.33	0.33	0.34

Notes:
[a]The F-values obtained through independent t-tests (Table 6-2) and ANOVA procedures (Table 6-3) indicate that none of the mean differences are statistically significant at $p < 0.05$.
[b]Average performance indicators, adjusted for industry effects and risk.

stay out of decision-making in the foreign affiliates. Like self-regulating systems, complex forms of MNEs may be better off when left on the "automatic" mode. In the MNEs that are the most diversified (both in terms of products and international markets), excessive interference from top managers at corporate headquarters can be counter-productive.

6.5 Concluding remarks

This chapter was designed to summarize the research findings of this research and to contribute to extend the discussion on current issues of international strategic management research. According to most industry observers, globalization will likely continue to escalate in importance over the next decade or longer, with considerable implications for companies and their decision-makers. Despite the lure of foreign markets, this research suggests that globalization may be expensive, not only in terms of duplicating and maintaining activities throughout the world, but also in terms of the top management's attention. Finding the appropriate level of attention that can be focused on global markets is a critical step towards establishing a clear positioning on the activity/attention matrix. Once this task is accomplished, MNEs can use the attention structures discussed in this research to influence managerial behaviors, and to ensure that such behaviors are supportive of intended objectives. In the final analysis, CEOs and members of the top management team need to be concerned not only with where and how they position activities on a worldwide basis – but with how they focus their own attention and that of their subordinates. Davenport and Beck (2001: 3) assert that "understanding and managing attention is now the single most important determinant of business success." For MNEs, getting globalization "right" represents an enormous challenge that is likely to grow larger everyday.

7
Conclusions and Limitations

This research's findings represent the early stage in the development of a body of empirical research addressing the issue of attention-management in MNEs. The principal ambition of this study is to use recent theory and research on attention to develop an understanding of the determinants and performance implications of a global mindset. In-depth field interviews were combined with the results of a cross-national survey of 136 MNEs to assist in the achievement of this research endeavor. This chapter reconciles the results presented in Chapter 6 with prior relevant literature in international strategic management research. Few research projects are without limitations, particularly when they address the inner functioning of medium and large MNEs worldwide. These limitations are discussed in this chapter, along with directions for future research.

7.1 Reconciliation with the prior literature on global mindset

This study uses a behavioral approach for understanding the global mindset phenomenon. This approach entails investigating how and why top managers allocate time, effort, and mental energy when analyzing global aspects of an MNE's environment. This type of research possesses important implications for theory because studies of the behaviors of top managers have been rare in strategic and international management literatures, particularly within multinational settings (Lohrke & Bruton, 1997; Pettigrew, 1992). For example, while researchers have often used the background characteristics of a top team, or features of its organizations to infer the presence (or absence) of a global mindset, few attempts have been made to actually measure the nature of the behaviors and cognitions of the top team. As a result, researchers may have overlooked important process variables and/or causal mechanisms.

By exploring the dynamics of top management *attention* in MNEs, the aim and hope of this research is to help remedy such neglect by initiating a stream of research that goes inside the "black box" of the global mindset phenomenon. Two particular insights from this study that are contrary to the traditional wisdom in the global mindset literature are worth highlighting.

Determinants of a global mindset

Rather than being simply a function of an MNE's administrative heritage or business environment, or reflecting the experience base of the individuals in question, the time and effort that the top team spends trying to make sense of international issues is explained primarily by the attention structures that an MNE puts in place. While other variables have some direct or indirect effect on the way top managers behave towards international issues, their importance is significantly less than the specific structures and processes that are developed to channel attention. Caution needs to be exercised when interpreting these findings though, since the structuring of organizational practices is often embedded in a company's heritage or the accumulated experience of top management. The findings suggest, however, that good principles of attention management are important to consider when shaping global mindsets because they mediate the relationship between objective properties of the MNE's environment of decisions and the allocation of attention by the top team.

Among attention structures, the concepts of structural positions and company resources do not appear to have great explanatory power by themselves. But the interview findings suggest that even these categories of attention structures complement others when shaping the nature of managerial behaviors. Structural positions, resources, incentives, and leadership development all join together towards explaining the formation of a global mindset. Therefore, researchers would be well advised to follow Van de Ven's (1979: 323) advice that to accurately describe complex research phenomena, "organizational forms must be joined together in a particular configuration to achieve completeness in a description of a social system, like pieces of a puzzle must be put together in certain ways to obtain a complete image." Subsequently, to understand the drivers of a global mindset, researchers cannot limit their investigations to the degree of international experience in a top team. On the contrary, this research points out to the need for considering a total system of variables pertaining to an MNE's organizational context.

It is also interesting to note that while this study focuses on identifying the structural determinants of a global mindset, many of the findings may be applicable to other topics relevant to strategic management as well. The identification and use of attention structures to focus employee attention on such things as technology absorption, customer satisfaction, and certain stakeholder benefits deserve particular scrutiny. Hence, the exploration of which attention structures are most effective in different scenarios, would lead to a significantly greater understanding of the extent and bases for differences in managerial behaviors across different organizations.

Performance implications

The findings of the research indicate that international attention may be in reality a mixed blessing. Previous research on global mindset suggests that the more global the mindset, the better the performance (Calof & Beamish, 1994; Murtha et al., 1998; Perlmutter, 1969). The findings in this study are consistent with this logic up to a point, but they also show that too little or too much attention to international issues can also be detrimental to performance. When things become too complex, top executives appear to be more effective if they can think quickly, and are confronted with a minimum input of information pertaining to international issues. Focusing on the essential is a key factor behind MNE success. For MNEs, getting the right level of attention focused on international issues constitutes a significant challenge. Chapter 6, however, highlighted several elements that provide perspective to the attention-performance relationship. These are summarized below:

1. Suggesting that top team members are often well-advised to focus the geographic scope of their scanning efforts does not mean that important issues occurring at the periphery of the world economy

should be neglected. While it entails significant costs in terms of short-term financial performance, the allocation of international attention by a company's top executives can be source of long-term advantages. Among other things, it could very well improve a company's ability to innovate and to react to unpredictable environments, as well as strengthen vital customer ties in distant locations. MNE top executives must weigh the relative importance of such benefits compared to short-term financial objectives.

2. In many cases, global thinking responsibilities can also be delegated. Issues occurring in distant and relatively unknown locations are often seen as low priority items on the agenda of busy MNE executives. But they may be worth (at least in terms of future returns expectations) the time and effort of middle managers. Dedicated units within the organization can be created to address emerging markets and to watch important trends worldwide. Delegation procedures have the merit of enhancing the future prospects of a company and simultaneously preserving the scarce attention of a company's top executives.

3. Finally, it is worth remembering that too much attention to international issues may no longer be representative of a true global mindset. Like expert drivers or musicians, truly effective managers must learn the difficult balance between paying attention to international issues and performing routine surveillance tasks. While attention is necessary to acquire the right perspective on things, and to develop skills that authorize the conduct of complex tasks, applying too much attention to anything also leads to a rigidity of thought that can interfere with effective performance (Nelson & Winter, 1982). This argument does not contradict the core assumption of this research that an attention-based perspective offers novel insights on the concept of global mindset. Managers with true cultural sensitivity will, on average, demonstrate global scanning, communication and decision-making behaviors that indicate their preoccupation with international business matters. However, the results suggest that excessive attention to international issues can be problematic in that it may also interfere with the development of a true global mindset.

The ideas presented in this research, particularly those pertaining to the relative performance of strategic archetypes associated with alternate strategies of globalization, are preliminary. Nevertheless, they have broader implications, especially in terms of strategy formulation. The global activity-attention matrix, for example, suggests that world-class competitors may be able to achieve global learning advantages without incurring the costs of duplicating activities around the world. Similarly, global sequential MNEs may be in a position to achieve global-scale economies and the benefits of international interdependence without incurring the burden of developing international attention in key managers. In addition, MNE operations may be effectively run and integrated across locations without excessive intervention from headquarters managers. This research was not designed to study the benefits and organizational requirements of complex global strategies. Instead, it sought to identify company practices that help understand whether and how top team members focus attention internationally. This research generates the following propositions that offer the focus for future research.

> *Research Proposition 1:* *Everything else being equal, world-class competitors will achieve higher performance levels than home-focused competitors.*
> *Research Proposition 2:* *Everything else being equal, global-sequential competitors will achieve higher performance levels than global-complex competitors.*
> *Research proposition 3:* *Everything else being equal, global-complex competitors will achieve the highest performance levels compared to other strategic archetypes provided certain resources and capabilities are in place.*

7.2 Implications for attention theory

The attention perspective developed in this research suggests several issues that organization studies might pursue. In particular, the basic findings underlying the drivers of managerial behaviors are fundamentally consistent with social theory perspectives (Ross & Nisbett, 1991). Specifically, the structures and systems that a firm puts in place explain the allocation of attention by individual and group decision-makers (March & Olsen, 1976; Ocasio, 1997). This study does not only support this view, it also adds to it by examining the relative influence exerted by various categories of attention regulators; namely structural positions, resources, incentives and leadership development activities.

An important contribution of this fine-grained analysis is to emphasize the symbolic nature of attention processing in organizations (Swidler, 1986). While theories of rational choice have often described the role of procedures, duty, tradition, and routines in explaining what decision-makers do, this research demonstrates that informal principles of actions – anchored for example around the notions of public recognition, career paths and vision statements – are meaningful elements to consider as well. By shaping what constitutes "appropriate behaviors", the symbolic features of an organization have important pragmatic and motivational implications for how decision-makers selectively focus their time and effort. They establish the logic (Jackall, 1988) or purpose (Bartlett & Ghoshal, 1994) against which choice situations are examined in a social context. Based on this insight, further research and theoretical developments are needed to construct a fully developed theory of how attention structures interact to affect the allocation of attention by decision-makers.

Despite the findings of current research, scholars often espouse a view of attention allocation that emphasizes the quasi-deterministic role of environmental influences, a key assumption of population ecology (Hannan & Freeman, 1977) and institutional theory (DiMaggio & Powell, 1983). Scott (1995), for example, argues that managerial cognitions and behaviors are the product of cultural and institutional processes occurring at varying levels of analysis, including the world economy, industry sectors, and organizations. Other perspectives emphasize the role of factors internal to decision-makers; namely background characteristics, skills and accumulated experiences (Hambrick & Mason, 1984). In contrast, garbage can views of organizations (Cohen, March, & Olsen, 1972; Cyert & March, 1963) emphasize the "fluid" or "stochastic" nature of attention processes.

The theory presented in this research reconciles these theoretical perspectives into an integrative and multi-level framework, which also extends Ocasio's (1997) original attention-based view of the firm in several distinct ways: First, this research describes a number of key mechanisms that explain whether, why and how a firm's top managers allocate attention to *international* issues. While Ocasio's work constituted a critical benchmark for this study, it was somewhat limited in its application to the issues at the center of our research. Ocasio acknowledges that his work does not represent a complete "theory" of attention management, nor does it speak directly to the myriad of issues associated with the specifics of international attention. As a consequence of this and the lack of supporting frameworks substantiated by other researchers, this research sought to extend Ocasio's work but it was also cautious in stretching it too far.

The results of this research also confirm the Hypothesis that attention structures partially mediate the relationship between a firm's environment of decisions and the allocation of attention by top managers. This finding is consistent with Weick's principle of enactment (Weick, 1979). Although industry and strategy considerations have no objective reality in the minds of decision-makers, their influence on attention processing is real, but indirect, operating through the structuring of organizational practices.

Finally, the perspective presented in this research has general implications for the ways in which scholars theorize about the origins of firm success. Traditionally, organization theorists have emphasized the inhibitory aspects of attention, which are well illustrated in the concept of bounded rationality, and the fact that any attention decision creates a departure from omniscient rationality. But Ocasio (1997: 203) also called attention to the adaptive properties of attention, which may facilitate the accuracy, speed and quality of complex information processing. By concentrating their mental energy, time and effort on a limited number of issues, activities and tasks, individual and group decision-makers can potentially invest resources in critical areas that facilitate successful strategic performance. The findings of this research illustrate both the inhibitory and positive effects of focused attention. By allocating attention to international issues, managers achieve benefits in areas that are critical to accurate planning and performance of MNEs. The scarce aspects of attention, however, necessarily imply that important trade-offs be made. Understanding the nature of these trade-offs require further research, theoretical developments, and empirical testing.

7.3   Measurement limitations

The use of survey questionnaires has inherent weaknesses. For example, given the difficulty associated with collecting primary data from senior executives, especially via a cross-national survey of MNEs, the study included only a single respondent within each company. This limitation creates the risk that the data obtained reflects the idiosyncratic perspectives of the respondent rather than top management-level or company-level data. To some extent, this problem was minimized by reliance on in-depth field interviews to augment the validity and interpretability of the questionnaire findings. Several validity checks were also reported in this research to ensure that the respondents provided reliable information. Nevertheless, other avenues, such as surveying multiple respondents within a top team and measuring the attentional behaviors of top managers via interviews, observations, or content analysis would also be fruitful.

Another measurement limitation is related to the difficulty of adequately measuring global mindsets, particularly at the top management-level of analysis. The approach used in this study measures the structures that channel information, and the behaviors of top managers that demonstrate their attention, but it does not attempt to map the cognitive processes that link them together. Previous research into cognitive mapping techniques (Calori et al., 1994; Huff, 1990) indicates a difficulty in measuring such processes, especially when the level of analysis is the entire top management team and the focus is the actual thoughts of individuals. Difficulties arise from the unstructured nature of managerial thoughts, which cannot be observed directly, and which are particularly complex for researchers, or managers themselves to recount or characterize accurately. In many cases, individuals may not be able to clearly articulate their ideas, and asking them a particular question can create a momentum that changes their attention focus. Similarly, much ambiguity still surrounds the bottom-up procedures that describe the manner in which individual-level properties manifest themselves at the level of an entire team. For example, is the mindset of top managers simply the sum of all individual top team members, or the summary result of complex compilation processes that describe a pattern of individual contributions on various tasks?

Recognizing these difficulties, this study relied on multiple measures of global mindset to tackle complex managerial behaviors that are presumably characteristic of the underlying overarching construct. The behaviors, which were identified through the course of in-depth field interviews with MNE managers, tap distinct and complementary facets of a global mindset. They constitute "configural unit properties" (Kozlowski & Klein, 2000) that derive from the cognitions and behaviors of individual team members but do not coalesce into highly consensual, shared group characteristics (i.e. top team members do not necessarily engage in identical behaviors). Thus, these properties should be considered as part of a total system rather than in isolation. Researchers relying on any one indicator, e.g. the amount of global scanning activity, would fail to establish a fully accurate portrayal of the global mindset phenomenon. Unfortunately, even with the use of multiple measures, it is likely that certain facets of the overarching global mindset construct have escaped observation. While the interviews revealed the importance of investigating scanning activities, the richness of communications with overseas managers, and the quality of decision-making procedures when operationalizing the amount of attention that a top team gives to international strategic issues, other important variables may also exist. While this issue must be noted as a limitation of this research, it represents a critical opportunity for future research on the topic of global mindsets.

This study's use of composite measures also warrants discussion. Chapter 5 reports a number of post-hoc analyses that describe the extent to which the results of a particular statistical test could be generalized across various individual measures. In some instances, the measures did align, thus providing clear support for the Hypothesis in question. However, in the majority of cases, discrepancies were noted across the measures. For example, while each of the three characteristics of the MNE's environment of decisions was found to impact the overall content of a firm's attention structures, it was not possible to find consistent results in the variables of the various attention structures. The global strategic posture, international interdependence, and international competition variables had distinct effects on the structuring of organizational practices. However, in no case, did the measures provide opposing evidence of support for a given research Hypothesis. It is useful to remember that in this research, the hypotheses were formulated at the level of latent (second-order) constructs. While this approach is typically necessary at such early stages of theory building, future research could attempt to provide a more complete theoretical rationale that would account for the observed differences in findings.

7.4 Role of international experience at the top

The results of this research indicate a limited impact of international experience on the attention of a company's top executives and on the choice of attention structures. While this finding makes theoretical sense (see Chapter 6), methodological caveats must be highlighted. In particular, the operationalization of international experience failed to capture elements such as whether MNE top executives have received an MBA degree or university training abroad. While these elements are essential to the education of modern international managers (Maisonrouge, 1983), they were not captured in this study. Thus it is possible that the domestically oriented educational backgrounds of managers may have contributed to their limited attention to international issues. More research is needed to investigate this possibility.

7.5 Direction of causality

Some of the relationships described in this study may involve reciprocal effects. For example, although it appears that expansive global strategic postures motivate the selection of the attention structures discussed in this study, an equally plausible argument can be made that, over time, the posture of a firm will also reflect the attention of its top managers (Hambrick & Mason, 1984). The existence of such feedback loops is consistent with Ocasio's (1997) framework in which mutually reinforcing relationships are described among environmental factors, attention structures, and decision-making behaviors. Furthermore, performance data was collected and averaged over a 5 year period, while all survey data (including data on attention variables) was collected in 2001/2002. This mismatch in dates introduces the possibility that international attention may be a consequence of performance rather than one of its predictor variables.

While the cross-sectional data employed in this research does not allow the utilization of procedures (such as lagged dependent variables) that would rule out such explanations, it is observed that mutually-reinforcing relationships may not be of equal strength, or occur simultaneously. In most organizations, a firm's environment of decisions will tend to have a more powerful effect on the cognitions and actions of top executives than vice-versa (Ashforth, 1989). Also, additional control variables were added to the models to estimate the impact of important prior conditions. This analysis confirmed that some of the causal paths depicted in Figure 3-2 were indeed being observed. For example, firm performance was found to be a likely outcome of differences in managerial behaviors rather than vice-versa. Nevertheless, future research should integrate more dynamic designs (e.g. longitudinal analysis and non-recursive statistical procedures) to more definitely establish the direction of causality in this research.

7.6   Sample bias

The selective focus of this study has been on the inner workings of MNEs with head-offices in the major world economies (USA, Canada, France, Germany, Japan, and the United Kingdom). A cross-national setting was chosen to address the call by researchers for more studies that focus on non-US contexts, and to reflect the fact that cultural factors are important drivers of a global mindset. However, this research did not address the practices of MNEs that have head-offices in emerging economies, or in countries traditionally known for their strong global orientations (e.g. Scandinavian countries). It may well be, however, that the type or relative effectiveness of attention structures, are different in these contexts. Similarly, no attempt was made to differentiate between different types of international attention, such as attention to well-established developed economies and attention to emerging markets. This omission suggests the need for more research in these areas.

As explained in Chapter 4, minimum-size criteria were also used to identify an adequate sampling frame. Indeed, ample evidence exists in international strategic management literature that the strategic imperatives – and resulting organizational requirements – of small MNEs may differ significantly from those of medium and large MNEs. As a result, the MNEs sampled in this research needed to be large enough to support the viability of the strategies and structures that were discussed. A possible problem with this approach is the potential for excessive restrictions in the range of global strategic postures and international interdependence levels of the MNEs being examined. As the study's results indicate, no statistical relationship was found between strategy variables and objective indicators of firm performance. One of the reasons for this result may be that this study's sample of MNEs was perhaps too homogenous in terms of the variables of interests. Broadening the range of organizations that would be eligible for inclusion in this study may facilitate the identification of more extreme strategies. It could also lead to the observation of greater differences in attention structures and mindset variables, thereby facilitating the testing of this study's hypotheses. But this enlarged sampling frame would also come at the cost of introducing potentially intrusive contingencies into the analysis. Hence, the disadvantages may well outweigh the advantages of this approach.

7.7   Levels of analysis

In discussing issues pertaining to global mindset and its appropriate level of analysis, it is important to note that the top team served as the focus of this study. Indeed, the questionnaire was designed to tap the managerial behaviors of top team members, and to identify factors that are significant drivers of such behaviors. Focusing on the top team level of analysis is consistent with a large body of international strategic management literature that argues that the greatest need for a global mindset exists at higher levels of an organization's hierarchy. This assumption was also supported by interview findings. Consequently, studying the determinants and performance of a global mindset at the top team-level of analysis is critical to improve our understanding of MNE practices and successes. Nevertheless, recent work in international strategic management literature also raises important questions about the appropriateness of limiting the unit of analysis to the top team. Clearly, a need exists for research that will integrate multiple levels of analysis (including individuals, groups, and entire organizations or industries) into their conceptualization of global mindsets. For example, Govindarajan and Gupta (2001: 124) observe:

> The value added by a global mindset, and the value subtracted by its absence, is likely to be strongest in the case of those individuals who are directly responsible for managing cross-border activities (for example the President of GE Lighting), followed by those who must interact frequently with colleagues from other countries. Nevertheless, if the company's goal is to capture and sustain global market leadership in its industry, it absolutely has to regard the development of a global mindset as a goal that encompasses each and every unit and each and every employee.

As already mentioned, a key measurement limitation of this research is that single key informants were used to estimate the behaviors of a company's top executives. The merits and potential shortcomings of this approach have been debated and discussed in strategic management literature (Huber & Power, 1985; Kumar et al., 1993). In this research, the use of a single key informant was deliberate, and necessary to build a cross national sample within the constraints of a fixed budget. Nevertheless, surveying multiple informants would allow the evaluation of the degree to which top executives achieve consensus on the attention variables that are discussed and measured in this research. Such an extension would be useful to evaluate the amount of measurement error attributable to different job responsibilities and areas of interest. Another avenue would be to determine how the attention of a top team emerges from the cognitions and actions of individual managers (Klein & Kozlowski, 2000). Top team members have different roles within the team, and thus, different attention foci (Hambrick & Mason, 1984). At this early stage of theory building, more research is needed to explain how these lower-unit properties interact to characterize the attention of the top team as a whole.

7.8 Static assessments of MNE practices

The theoretical underpinnings of this study are built on the notion that MNEs continually adapt the content of attention structures in response to signals from the environment of decisions in the hope of influencing managerial behaviors and overall performance levels. While this study has focused on explaining the nature of the relationships involving these variables, no attempt was made to discuss and measure related issues of process. As such, this study is based on a static assessment of global strategic postures, international strategies, and international competition variables. The dynamic relationships that exist between these changing variables and the structuring of organizational practices by an MNE are not addressed. The attention structures identified in the study reflect the existing functioning of organizations. No indication is made of the specific paths that were followed by MNEs in selecting such structures. Moreover, the intermediary role that implementation skills play in the linkage between attention structures and managerial behaviors is not discussed in this study. Clearly, these problems constitute fertile ground for further research.

Other issues of process that offer a potentially interesting ground for future research center on the role of the board of directors. The interview findings made apparent that the development of global mindsets within MNEs constitutes an issue that necessitates the board's direct attention. In this study, additional analyses were conducted to determine whether board-level variables such as size, tenure, and proportion of outsiders or stockholders, would affect the level of attention that MNE top executives invest to make sense of international strategic issues, or the choice of attention structures, but no such effects were found. Thus, a promising area for future research concerns the impact, if any, that various board characteristics have on the relationships investigated in this research.

7.9   A universal model of global mindset

Finally, this study followed an MNE approach to the global mindset phenomenon. Organizations were excluded from this analysis if they did not have operations in more than two countries. The value of a global mindset, and the applicability of the research hypotheses have not been examined in a strictly domestic context. However, this study recognizes that virtually all companies, regardless of industry or strategy differences, are increasingly faced with the human challenges of globalization, and the need for managers who can think across borders (Doz et al., 2001). Ideally, future research would need to extend the theory of global mindset suggested in this study to a strategic management research across a broad spectrum of possible domestic and international contexts.

Appendix A: Overview of the Research Methodology

A multi-phase, multi-method research approach was chosen to investigate this study's research questions (Figure A-1). This approach involved a phase of exploratory research, followed by theory testing, and finally, post-hoc confirmatory research. As observed by Parkhe (1993: 256), ongoing theory advancement, especially in nascent areas of enquiry, requires "continuous interplay between deductive and inductive, theory testing and theory generation ... because these approaches complement and reinforce each other." The three research phases are now briefly described in turn.

Phase 1: After carefully reviewing the attention-based literature in three key disciplines of cognitive psychology, micro-economics, and organization theory, semi-structured, probing field interviews were conducted. These interviews were designed to improve our understanding of how companies of various sizes and in a range of industries approach the global mindset imperative. In total, eighteen senior executives in thirteen different MNEs were interviewed. This grounded theory approach was undertaken to confirm the practical relevance of global mindsets, to clarify the construct's domain, and to develop research propositions that map the determinants and performance implications of a global mindset.

Phase 2: The next phase of the research was focused on hypothesis testing and external validity. This quantitative study of MNE practices involved mailing a questionnaire to a cross-national sample of 900 medium and large MNEs headquartered in 6 different countries (USA, Canada, Japan, France, Germany, and the United Kingdom) across a wide spectrum of industries. The questionnaire was subjected to intensive pre-testing to ensure face validity and to eliminate obvious problems of clarity in the wording of specific questionnaire items. The data obtained through this mail survey was then subjected to rigorous multivariate analyses to test the research propositions formulated in Phase 1.

Phase 3: Following the mail survey and the statistical analyses, follow-up interviews with ten senior executives in nine different MNEs were used to shed light on quantitative data, to validate results, and to assist in the interpretation of the study's findings. The objective was to verify whether current managerial perspectives supported the conclusions that were drawn from the statistical analyses. This triangulation between the questionnaire and the pre and post test interview data led to the construction of a rich database that offered critical insights on the determinants and the performance implications of global mindsets.

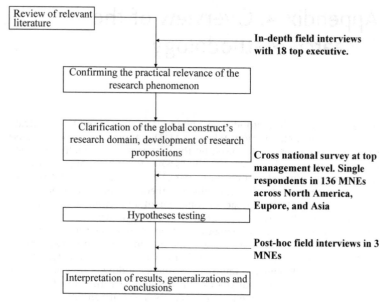

Figure A-1   Research Process

Appendix B: Validity Checks

It was important to test the validity of the questionnaire data to ensure that various sources of method biases do not constitute a major concern in this database. Table B-1 shows the means, standard deviations, and inter-correlations for all variables. A comparison of differences in the mean values of the responding and nonresponding companies based on sales revenues, assets, company age, number of employees, average performance, and proportion of foreign sales to total sales did not reveal any significant nonresponse bias. The largest responding and nonresponding companies had annual sales of $152 billion and $179 billion, respectively, and the smallest responding and nonresponding companies both had annual sales revenues of approximately $26.0 million. The average sales of the two groups were $5.3 billion and $3.8 billion, respectively. The proportional breakdown of respondents by industry and country also paralleled that of the initial group, with about half of the responding companies located in North America (USA and Canada), 20 percent in Japan, and the remaining in Western Europe.

For data collection, the key informant approach was adopted, whose merits and shortcomings have been debated in strategic management literature (Huber & Power, 1985; Kumar, Stern, & Anderson, 1993; Seidler, 1974). While the ideal may be to triangulate data through the use of multiple informants, it is difficult to identify and collect primary data from multiple senior-level executives in a cross national sample of MNEs (Doty, Glick, & Huber, 1993). Nonetheless, in 28 of the 136 companies, we obtained data from two informants as a validation sample, and calculated Kappa coefficients to assess within-company agreement on each of the study's key constructs. Kappa is a correlation coefficient that corrects for the expected level of correlation between raters (Westphal, 1999). The value of kappa coefficients ranged between .68 and .92, and the overall kappa was .78 indicating good to excellent agreement beyond chance according to criteria set forth by Fleiss (1981).

The validity of the informants' responses was further checked in two ways. First, informants were asked to indicate their current job titles in the organization. Of the informants, 53 percent held the title of CEO, CFO or COO, 17 percent held the title of Senior Vice-President or President, and 30 percent held the title of General Manager or Director. Therefore, the sample included informants that represented the concept of a dominant coalition (Cyert & March, 1963) suggesting they were likely to be knowledgeable about the issues under study.

Second, a comparison was made between the correlations between data reported by the informants with secondary sources of data on key internationalization variables such as the ratios of foreign sales to total sales, foreign

141

Table B-1 Correlations, Means and Standard Deviations[a]

	Mean	S.D.	1	2	3	4	5	6	7	8	9	10	11	12	13
1. US dummy	.34	.47													
2. Firm age	56.00	39.80	-.19												
3. Firm size	1.56	1.79	-.17	.39											
4. R&D intensity	7.49	19.33	-.02	-.22	-.21										
5. Diversification	.78	.43	-.02	.16	.33	.02									
6. Size of top group	5.54	3.87	-.02	.05	.52	-.03	.17								
7. International experience at the top	1.69	2.45	.03	.02	.30	.23	.19	.25							
8. Cultural heterogeneity at the top	2.68	2.10	-.20	.03	.15	.05	.03	-.02	.27						
9. Global strategic posture	1.37	.68	-.21	.10	.28	.10	.17	.07	.34	.37					
10. International interdependence	25.84	5.89	.09	.20	.39	.02	.23	.29	.34	.17	.41				
11. International competition	4.65	1.16	-.16	-.03	.04	.06	.13	.01	.00	-.05	.13	.00			
12. Attention structures index	.00	1.00	-.02	-.03	.09	.05	.09	.18	.26	.09	.37	.37	.29		
13. International attention index	.00	1.00	-.19	.05	.26	.21	.05	.12	.30	.30	.56	.35	.18	.66	
14. Firm performance	-.88	2.33	.21	.06	.02	-.22	-.02	-.17	-.00	-.03	-.08	.00	-.02	-.03	-.16

[a] $n = 136$. Correlations greater than 0.17 are significant at $p < .05$, and those greater than 0.22 are significant at $p < 0.01$.

assets to total assets, and number of countries in which the company maintains operations. The correlation coefficients ranged in values from .8 to .9 (p < .05). These correlations, along with the results from the subsample with multiple informants increased our confidence in the quality and accuracy of our data.

With regard to the possibility of common method variance, a post hoc procedure suggested by Podsakoff and Organ (1986) was employed to assess the extent of common method variance. Responses to survey items for all variables were pooled and subjected to principal component analysis, which yielded fourteen factors with eigenvalues greater than 1.0, while no general factor was apparent in the un-rotated factor structure, with factor 1 accounting for only 19 percent of the variance. This indicates that common method bias was not operating at a level that would seriously distort the findings in this study.

Appendix C: Profiles of Key Attention Behavior Variables

This appendix presents brief profiles of top team-level behaviors derived from descriptive statistics computed from the questionnaire data.

Industry differences. The profiles of international attention were relatively similar across the 13 selected industries. In particular, analysis of variance (ANOVA) was used to determine whether the overall amount of attention that MNE top executives paid to international issues varied according to industry, but none of the noted differences were significant at the $p < 0.05$ level (Table C-1). In fact, all industries were within one standard deviation either below or above the sample mean in terms of the amount of attention that was paid to international strategic issues.

When the dependent variable was disaggregated into four separate measures representing distinct facets of attention to international issues (scanning, media, CEO travel, decision-making), similarities across industries became clear (see Table C-1). Nevertheless, while the industry differences were not statistically significant in this database, the group sizes were unequal. As a result, several dissimilarities that exist across broad industry sectors require discussion. Six industries appeared to pay more attention to international issues than the sample mean: pharmaceutical, communications equipment, electrical equipment, motor vehicles and parts, software, and industrial machinery. Conversely, seven industries appeared to pay relatively less attention to international issues than the sample mean. These industries are food products, semi-conductors, building products, metals, computers, chemicals, and scientific instruments. These findings reflect the view that different industries face distinct pressures for local responsiveness, global integration, and learning across borders, leading them to vary somewhat in the amount of attention that their top teams pay to international strategic issues (Ghoshal, 1987; Prahalad & Doz, 1987).

Country differences. The profiles of international attention were significantly different across the countries represented in this sample (see Table C-2). Specifically, top executives in countries from Western Europe (France, Germany, and the United Kingdom) pay significantly greater amounts of attention to international issues compared to top executives in North America or Japan. Specifically, France is distinguished as the country that demonstrates the most attention to international issues. Conversely, the lowest scores on the international attention variable were obtained by companies in the United States and Japan, suggesting executives in these countries are more preoccupied by domestic issues and events than they are focused on international issues.

Table C-1 International Attention in Thirteen Industries

	Overall Index	Global Scanning	Media	Amount of CEO Travel	Decision-Making
Food products (n = 6)	-.77	3.44	4.55	13.50	3.39
Semi-conductors (n = 7)	-.56	3.48	4.59	22.14	3.38
Building products (n = 3)	-.34	3.44	4.90	18.33	4.00
Metals (n = 14)	-.33	3.69	4.86	20.36	3.71
Computers (n = 4)	-.19	3.75	4.27	22.50	4.67
Chemicals (n = 16)	-.07	3.60	4.81	25.69	4.27
Scientific instruments (n = 11)	-.03	3.67	4.93	21.73	4.52
Industrial machinery (n = 24)	.09	3.89	5.10	24.54	4.26
Software (n = 13)	.16	3.87	5.04	30.00	4.18
Motor vehicles and parts (n = 13)	.22	4.62	5.01	23.38	4.67
Electrical equipment (n = 13)	.22	4.79	4.85	28.46	3.85
Communications equipment (n = 8)	.45	4.17	4.94	27.63	5.13
Pharmaceuticals (n = 4)	.65	3.83	5.13	45.00	4.58
F-Value	1.09	1.31	.42	1.18	1.42
Significance[a]	.37	.22	.95	.30	.17

[a] n = 136. All industry mean differences are statistically non-significant at $p < 0.05$.

Table C-2 International Attention in Six Countries

	Overall Index	Global Scanning	Media	Amount of CEO Travel	Decision-Making
United States (n = 46)	-.27	3.49	4.83	21.04	4.08
Japan (n = 25)	-.25	4.36	4.66	16.68	3.84
Canada (n = 24)	-.11	3.94	4.80	22.88	4.04
United Kingdom (n = 16)	.47	3.56	5.18	36.56	4.81
Germany (n = 10)	.52	4.50	5.35	29.50	4.37
France (n = 15)	.57	4.56	5.10	37.07	4.24
F-Value	3.56	3.53	1.305	6.622	1.532
Significance[a]	.00	.00	.27	.00	.18

[a] $n = 136$

Table C-3   International Attention Across Company Clusters[a]

	Strategic Cluster 1	Strategic Cluster 2	T-Value
Global strategic posture	.98	1.84	9.30***
International interdependence	22.97	29.27	7.33***
International competition	4.64	4.65	.04
International experience at the top	.59	3.00	6.51***
Cultural heterogeneity at the top	1.58	3.98	8.05***
International content of attention structures	−.39	.47	5.53***
	n = 54	N = 46	
	37.5%	62.5%	
International Activity in Cluster	MODERATE	HIGH	
International Attention			
Overall Index	−.49	.58	−7.33***
Scanning	3.72	4.18	−2.20*
Media	4.59	5.28	−4.52***
CEO travel	17.80	33.12	−6.27***
Decision-making	3.69	4.71	−7.33***

Significance of difference in means, $^\dagger p < 0.10$; $^* p < 0.05$; $^{**} p < 0.01$; $^{***} p < 0.001$

Company differences. Important differences of attentional behaviors were also found across companies. A two-step cluster analysis procedure was used to group MNEs according to some measure of homogeneity. In this case, the sample of MNEs was partitioned according to the expansiveness of their global strategic posture, the interdependence of their international operations, the degree of international competition prevailing within the industry, the international content of their attention structures, and the international composition of their top management team. The "best" number of natural groupings of firms within this data set was determined using the Log-likelihood "distance" between cluster means, and the Schwarz's Bayesian criterion. Two groups were created. The first cluster comprised companies that experience moderate levels of international activity, while the second one corresponded to a context of high international activity. The results of this procedure are shown in Table C-3. Post hoc independent T-tests showed that the amount of attention that a top team gives to international issues is consistently greater in the case of firms that operate in strategic cluster 2, where the intensity of international activity is the highest. Therefore, the company factors included in the cluster analysis appear to have an impact (in some direct or indirect ways) on the attentional behaviors of a company's top team.

References

Adler, N. J., & Bartholomew, S. 1992. Managing globally competent people. *Academy of Management Executive*, 6(3): 52–65.

Aiken, L. S., & West, S. G. 1991. *Multiple regression: testing and interpreting regressions*. London: Sage Publications.

Argyris, C. 1976. Single-loop and double-loop models in research on decision making. *Administrative Science Quarterly*, 21(3): 363–375.

Ashforth, B. E. 1989. The experience of powerlessness in organizations. *Organizational Behavior and Human Decision Processes*, 43: 207–242.

Athanassiou, N., & Nigh, D. 2000. Internationalization, tacit knowledge, and the top management teams of MNEs. *Journal of International Business Studies*, 31(3): 471–487.

Baron, R. M., & Kenny, D. A. 1986. The moderator-mediator variable distinction in social psychological research: conceptual, strategic and statistical considerations. *Journal of Personality and Social Psychology*, 51: 1173–1182.

Bartlett, C. A., & Ghoshal, S. 1986. Tap Your Subsidiaries for Global Reach. *Harvard Business Review*, 64: 87–94.

Bartlett, C. A., & Ghoshal, S. 1989. *Managing across borders: the transnational solution*. Boston: Harvard Business School Press.

Bartlett, C. A., & Ghoshal, S. 1994. Changing the role of top management: beyond strategy to purpose. *Harvard Business Review*, November–December: 79–88.

Bartunek, J. M., Gordon, J. R., & Weathersby, R. P. 1983. Developing "complicated" understanding in administrators. *Academy of Management Review*, 8(2): 273–284.

Berlyne, D. E. 1970. Attention as a problem in behavior theory. In D. I. Mostofsky (ed.), *Attention: Contemporary theory and analysis*: 25–49. New York: Appleton-Century-Crofts.

Birkinshaw, J., & Fry, N. 1998. Subsidiary initiatives to develop new markets. *Sloan Management Review*, 39(3): 51–61.

Birkinshaw, J., Morrison, A., & Hulland, J. 1995. Structural and competitive determinants of a global integration strategy. *Strategic Management Journal*, 16(8): 637–655.

Black, S., Gregersen, H., Mendenhall, M., & Stroh, L. 1999a. *Globalizing people through international assignments*. Reading, MA: Addison-Wesley.

Black, S., Morrison, A., & Gregersen, H. 1999b. *Global explorers: the next generation of leaders*. New York: Routledge.

Bollen, K., & Lennox, R. 1991. Conventional wisdom on measurement: A structural equation perspective. *Psychological Bulletin*, 88(3): 588–606.

Briggs, S. R., & Cheek, J. M. 1986. The role of factor analysis in the development and evaluation of personality scales. *Journal of Personality*, 54(1): 106–148.

Broadbent, D. E. 1958. *Perception and communication.* Oxford: Pergamon Press.

Burgelman, R. A. 1983a. A model of the interaction of strategic behavior, corporate context, and the concept of strategy. *Academy of Management Review,* 8(1): 61–70.

Burgelman, R. A. 1983b. A process model of internal corporate venturing in the diversified major firm. *Administrative Science Quarterly,* 28(2): 223–244.

Butterfield, K. D., Trevino, L. K., & Ball, G. A. 1996. Punishment from the manager's perspective: a grounded investigation and inductive model. *Academy of Management Journal,* 39(6): 1479–1512.

Calof, J. L., & Beamish, P. W. 1994. The right attitude for international success. *Ivey Business Quarterly,* 59(1): 105–110.

Calori, R., Johnson, G., & Sarnin, P. 1994. CEO's cognitive maps and the scope of the organization. *Strategic Management Journal,* 15(6): 437–457.

Capron, L. 1999. The long-term performance of horizontal acquisitions. *Strategic Management Journal,* 20(11): 987–1018.

Carpenter, M. A., & Fredrickson, J. W. 2001. Top management teams, global strategic posture, and the moderating role of uncertainty. *Academy of Management Journal,* 44(3): 533–545.

Carpenter, M. A., Sanders, W. G., & Gregersen, H. B. 2001. Bundling human capital with organizational context: The impact of international assignment experience on multinational firm performance and CEO pay. *Academy of Management Journal,* 44(3): 493–511.

Cattel, R. B. 1965. *The scientific analysis of personality.* New York: Penguin Books.

Caves, R. E. 1996. *Multinational enterprise and economic analysis* (2nd ed.). Cambridge, MA: Cambridge University Press.

Chandler, A. D. 1970. *Strategy and structure.* Cambridge: M.I.T. Press.

Cohen, M. D., March, J. M., & Olsen, J. P. 1972. A garbage can model of organizational choice. *Administrative Science Quarterly,* 17(1): 1–24.

Conference Board. 1999. Globalizing the board of directors: Trends and strategies.

Cook, R. D., & Weisberg, S. 1982. *Residuals and influence in regression.* New York: Chapman and Hall.

Coval, J. D., & Moskowitz, T. J. 1999. Home bias at home: local equity preference in domestic portfolios. *Journal of Finance,* 54(6): 2045–2073.

Cowan, D. A. 1986. Developing a process model of problem recognition. *Academy of Management Review,* 11(4): 763–776.

Cyert, R. M., & March, J. G. 1963. *A behavioral theory of the firm.* Englewood Cliffs, N.J: Prentice-Hall.

Czernich, C., & Zander, U. 2000. *Exploring exploration: Attention as hunting, gathering and farming in MNEs.* Paper presented at the Academy of International Business Annual Meeting, Phoenix.

Daft, R. L., & Lengel, R. H. 1986. Organizational information requirements, media richness and structural design. *Management Science,* 32(5): 554–571.

Daily, C. M., Certo, S. T., & Dalton, D. R. 2000. International experience in the executive suite: the path to prosperity. *Strategic Management Journal*, 21(4): 515–523.

D'Aveni, R., & MacMillan, I. C. 1990. Crisis and the content of managerial communications: A study of the focus of attention of top managers in surviving and failing firms. *Administrative Science Quarterly*, 35(4): 634–657.

Davenport, T. H., & Beck, J. C. 2001. *The attention economy*. Boston: Harvard Business School Press.

Day, D. L. 1994. Raising radicals: Different processes for championing innovative corporate ventures. *Organization Science*, 5(2): 148–172.

Deaborne, D. C., & Simon, H. 1958. Selective perception: a note on the departmental identification of executives. *Sociometry*, 21: 140–144.

Deutsch, J. A., & Deutsch, D. 1963. Attention: Some theoretical considerations. *Psychological Review*, 70(1): 51–61.

DiMaggio, P. J., & Powell, W. W. 1983. The iron cage revisited: Institutional isomorphism and collective rationality in organizational fields. *American Sociological Review*, 48(2): 147–160.

Doty, D. H., Glick, W. H., & Huber, G. P. 1993. Fit, equifinality, and organizational effectiveness: a test of two configurational theories. *Academy of Management Journal*, 36(6): 1196–1250.

Doz, Y. L., & Prahalad, C. K. 1991. Managing DMNEs: A search for a new paradigm. *Strategic Management Journal*, 12 (Summer Special Issue): 145–164.

Doz, Y. L., Santos, J., & Williamson, P. 2001. *From global to metanational: how companies win in the knowledge economy*. Boston: Harvard Business School Press.

Drucker, P. F. 1993. *Post capitalist society* (1st ed.). New York: HarperBusiness.

Drucker, P. F. 1999. *Management challenges for the 21st century* (1st ed.). New York: HarperBusiness.

Dunning, J. H. 1974. *Economic analysis and the multinational enterprise*. London: Allen & Unwin.

Dunning, J. H. 1988. The eclectic paradigm of international production: a restatement and some possible extensions. *Journal of International Business Studies*, 19(1): 1–31.

Dunning, J. H. 1996. The geographical sources of competitiveness of firms: some results from a new survey. *Transnational Corporations*, 5(3): 1–30.

Dutton, J. E., & Duncan, R. B. 1987. The creation of momentum for change through the process of strategic issue diagnosis. *Strategic Management Journal*, 8(3): 279–295.

Dutton, J. E., Fahey, L., & Narayanan, V. K. 1983. Toward understanding strategic issue diagnosis. *Strategic Management Journal*, 4(4): 307–323.

Earley, P. C. 2000. Creating hybrid team cultures: an empirical test of transnational team functioning. *Academy of Management Journal*, 43(1): 26–49.

Epstein, S. 1983. Aggregation and beyond: Some basic issues on the prediction of behavior. *Journal of Personality*, 51(3): 360–392.

Fayerweather, J. 1969. *International business management: A conceptual framework.* New York: McGraw-Hill.

Garg, V. K., Walters, B. A., & Priem, R. L. 2003. Chief executive scanning emphases, environmental dynamism, and manufacturing firm performance. *Strategic Management Journal*, 24(8): 725–744.

Garten, J. E. 1997. *The big ten: the big emerging markets and how they will change our lives* (1st ed.). New York: BasicBooks.

Ghoshal, S. 1987. Global strategy: An organizing framework. *Strategic Management Journal*, 8(5): 425–440.

Ghoshal, S., & Bartlett, Christopher A. 1988. Creation, adoption and diffusion of innovations by subsidiaries of multinational corporations. *Journal of International Business Studies*, 19(3): 365–388.

Ghoshal, S., & Kim, S. K. 1986. Building effective intelligence systems for competitive advantage. *Sloan Management Review*, 28(1): 49–58.

Ghoshal, S., & Westney, E. D. 1991. Organizing competitor analysis systems. *Strategic Management Journal*, 12(1): 17–31.

Gifford, S. 1992. Allocation of entrepreneurial attention. *Journal of Economic Behavior and Organization*, 19: 265–284.

Glaser, B. G., & Strauss, A. L. 1967. *The discovery of grounded theory.* Chicago: Aldine Publishing Company.

Gomes-Mejia, L. R., & Palich, L. E. 1997. Cultural diversity and the performance of multinational firms. *Journal of International Business Studies*, 28(2): 309–335.

Govindarajan, V., & Gupta, A. K. 1998. Setting a course for the new global landscape. *Financial Times*, 30 Jan.

Govindarajan, V., & Gupta, A. K. 2001. *The quest for global dominance: transforming global presence into global competitive advantage.* San Francisco: Jossey-Bass.

Green, S., Hassan, F., Immelt, J., Marks, M., & Meiland, D. 2003. In search of global leaders. *Harvard Business Review*, 81(8): 38–43.

Gupta, A. K., & Govindarajan, V. 2002. Cultivating a global mindset. *Academy of Management Executive*, 16(1): 116–126.

Gupta, V., & Govindarajan, A. K. 2001. Converting global presence into global competitive advantage. *Academy of Management Journal*, 15(2): 45–58.

Hambrick, D. C., & Mason, P. 1984. Upper echelons: the organization as a reflection of its top managers. *Academy of Management Review*, 9(2): 193–206.

Hamel, G., & Prahalad, C. K. 1985. Do you really have a global strategy? *Harvard Business Review*, July–August: 139–148.

Hannan, M. T., & Freeman, J. 1977. The population ecology of organizations. *American Journal of Sociology*, 82(5): 929–964.

Hansen, M. T., & Haas, M. R. 2001. Competing for attention in knowledge markets: electronic document dissemination in a management consulting company. *Administrative Science Quarterly*, 46(1): 1–28.

Harzing, A. W. 2000. Cross national industrial mail surveys: why do response rates differ between countries. *Industrial Marketing Management*, 29(3): 243–254.

Hedlund, G. 1986. The hypermodern MNE: a heterarchy? *Human Resource Management*, 25(1): 9–35.

Heenan, D. A., & Perlmutter, H. V. 1979. *Multinational organization development*. Reading, Mass.: Addison-Wesley Pub. Co.

Hitt, M. A., Hoskisson, R. E., & Kim, H. 1997. International diversification: Effects on innovation and firm performance in product-diversified firms. *Academy of Management Journal*, 40(4): 767–798.

Hoffman, A. J., & Ocasio, W. 2001. Not all events are attended equally: Toward a middle range theory of industry attention to external events. *Organization Science*, 12(4): 414–434.

Hoffman, R. C., & Gopinath, C. 1994. The importance of international business to the strategic agenda of U.S. CEOs. *Journal of International Business Studies*, 25(3): 625–637.

Hofstede, G. H. 1980. *Culture's consequences, international differences in work-related values*. Beverly Hills, CA: Sage Publications.

Hout, T., Porter, M. E., & Rudden, E. 1982. How global companies win out? *Harvard Business Review*, September–October: 98–108.

Huber, G. P., & Power, D. J. 1985. Retrospective reports on strategic-level managers: guidelines for increasing their efficiency. *Strategic Management Journal*, 6(2): 171–180.

Huff, A. S. 1990. *Mapping strategic thought*. Chichester: Wiley.

Hymer, S. H. 1976. *The international operations of national firms: A study of direct investment*. Cambridge: MIT Press.

Jackall, R. 1988. *Moral mazes: The world of corporate managers*. New York, NY: Oxford University Press.

James, W. 1890. *The principles of psychology*. New York: Dover Publications.

Jeannet, J.-P. 2000. *Managing with a global mindset*. London: Prentice Hall.

Johanson, J., & Vahlne, J. E. 1977. The internationalization process of the firm: A model of knowledge development and increasing foreign market commitments. *Journal of International Business Studies*, 8(1): 23–32.

Johnson, S. 2003. Mind share. *Wired Magazine*. http://www.wired.com/wired/archive/11.06/blog_spc.html

Kahneman, D. 1973. *Attention and effort*. Englewood Cliffs: Prentice-Hall.

Kahneman, D., & Treisman, A. 1984. Changing views of attention and automaticity. In R. Parasuraman, & D. R. Davies (eds), *Varieties of attention*. New York: Academic Press.

Kanter, R. M. 1994. What thinking globally really means. In P. Barnevik, & R. M. Kanter (eds), *Global strategies: Insights from the world's leading thinkers*. Boston: Harvard Business School Press.

Kanter, R. M. 1995. *World class: thriving locally in the global economy*. New York: Simon & Schuster.

Keegan, W. J. 1974. Multinational scanning: a study of the information sources utilized by headquarters executives in multinational companies. *Administrative Science Quarterly*, 19(3): 411–421.

Kiesler, S., & Sproull, L. 1982. Managerial response to changing environments: Perspectives on problem sensing from social cognition. *Administrative Science Quarterly*, 27(4): 548–570.

Kim, W. C., & Mauborgne, R. A. 1993. Procedural justice, attitudes, and subsidiary top management compliance with multinationals' corporate strategic decisions. *Academy of Management Journal*, 36(3): 502–256.

Klein, K. J., & Kozlowski, S. W. J. 2000. *Multilevel theory, research, and methods in organizations: foundations, extensions, and new directions* (1st ed.). San Francisco: Jossey-Bass.

Kobrin, S. J. 1994. Is there a relationship between a geocentric mindset and multinational strategy? *Journal of International Business Studies*, 25(3): 493–512.

Kostova, T. 1999. Transnational transfer of strategic organizational practices: A contextual perspective. *Academy of Management Review*, 24(2): 308–324.

Kozlowski, S. W. J., & Klein, K. J. 2000. A multilevel approach to theory and research in organizations. In K. J. Klein, & S. W. J. Kozlowski (eds), *Multilevel theory, research, and methods in organizations: Foundations, extensions, and new directions*: xxix, 605. San Francisco: Jossey-Bass.

Kumar, N., Stern, L. W., & Anderson, J. C. 1993. Conducting interorganizational research using key informants. *Academy of Management Journal*, 36(6): 1633.

Laberge, D. 1995. *Attentional processing: The brain's art of mindfulness*. Cambridge, Mass.: Harvard University Press.

Laberge, D., & Samuels, S. J. 1974. Toward a theory of automatic information processing in reading. *Cognitive psychology*, 6(2): 293–323.

Lachman, R., Lachman, J. L., & Butterfield, E. 1979. *Cognitive psychology and information processing: An introduction*. New York: Lawrence Erlbaum Associates.

Langer, E. J. 1989. Minding matters: The consequences of mindlessness-mindfulness. In L. Berkowitz (ed.), *Advances in Experimental Social Psychology*, Vol. 22: 132–173.

Langley, A. 1995. Between 'paralysis by analysis' and 'extinction by instinct'. *Sloan Management Review*, 36(3): 63–76.

Leonard Barton, D. 1992. Core capabilities and core rigidities: A paradox in managing new product development. *Strategic Management Journal*, 13 (Summer Special Issue): 111–125.

Levitt, B., & March, J. G. 1995. Chester I. Barnard and the intelligence of learning. In O. E. Williamson (ed.), *Organization theory: From Chester Barnard to the present and beyond*: 11–37. Oxford: Oxford University Press.

Locke, K. 2001. *Grounded theory in management research*. London: Sage Publications.

Logan, G. D. 1980. Attention and automaticity in Stroop and priming tasks: Theory and data. *Cognitive Psychology*, 12(4): 523–553.

Lohrke, F. T., & Bruton, G. D. 1997. Contributions and gaps in international strategic management literature. *Journal of International Management*, 3(1): 25–57.

Louis, M. R., & Sutton, R. L. 1991. Switching cognitive gears: From habits of mind to active thinking. *Human Relations*, 44(1): 55–76.

Lyles, M. A. 1990. A research agenda for strategic management in the 1990s. *Journal of Management Studies*, 27(4): 363–375.

Maisonrouge, J. G. 1983. The education of a modern international manager. *Journal of International Business Studies*, Spring/Summer: 141–146.

March, J. G. 1994. *A primer on decision making: How decisions happen*. New York, NY: The Free Press.

March, J. G., & Olsen, J. P. 1976. *Ambiguity and choice in organizations*. Bergen: Universitetsforlaget.

March, J. G., & Simon, H. A. 1958. *Organizations*. New York, NY: Wiley.

Marschak, J., & Radner, R. 1972. *Economic theory of teams*. New Haven: Yale University Press.

McCall, M. W., & Kaplan, R. E. 1985. *Whatever it takes: Decision makers at work*. Englewood Cliffs, N.J: Prentice-Hall.

McCallum, J. 1995. National borders matter: Canada-U.S. regional trade patterns. *American Economic Review*, 85(3): 615–623.

McLuhan, M. 1965. *Understanding media: The extensions of man*. New York: McGraw-Hill Book Co.

Miller, G. A. 1956. The magical number seven plus or minus two: Some limits on our capacity for processing information. *Psychological Review*, 63: 81–97.

Moray, N. 1969. *Listening and attention*. Harmondsworth: Penguin.

Morrison, A., Beck, J. & Bouquet, C. 2004. "Globalization and management attention", in Chowdhury, S. (ed.), *Next Generation Business Handbook*. New York: John Wiley & Sons.

Morrison, A., Bouquet, C., & Beck, J. 2004. Netchising: the next global wave? *Long Range Planning*, 37: 11–27.

Murtha, T. P., Lenway, S. A., & Bagozzi, R. P. 1998. Global mindsets and cognitive shifts in a complex multinational corporation. *Strategic Management Journal*, 19(2): 97–114.

Neisser, U. 1976. *Cognition and reality*. San Francisco: W. H. Freeman.

Nelson, R. R., & Winter, S. G. 1982. *An evolutionary theory of economic change*. Cambridge, MA: Harvard University Press.

Norman, D. A. 1969. *Memory and attention: An introduction to human information processing*. New York: Wiley.

Nunnally, J. C., & Bernstein, I. H. 1994. The theory of measurement error. In J. V. a. J. R. Belser (ed.), *Psychometric theory*, Third ed.: 211–247. New York: McGraw-Hill, Inc.

Ocasio, W. 1997. Towards an attention-based view of the firm. *Strategic Management Journal*, 18 (Summer Special Issue): 187–206.

Ohmae, K. 1989. Managing in a borderless world. *Harvard Business Review*, 89(3): 152–161.

Palepu, K. 1985. Diversification strategy, profit performance and the entropy measure. *Strategic Management Journal*, 6(3): 239–255.

Parkhe, A. 1993. "Messy " methodological predispositions, and theory development in international joint ventures. *Academy of Management Review*, 18(2): 227–268.

Passino, J. H., & Severance, D. G. 1990. Harnessing the potential of information technology for support of the new global organization. *Human Resource Management*, 29(1): 69–76.

Pavlov, I. P. 1960. *Conditioned reflexes: An investigation of the physiological activity of the cerebral cortex*. New York: Dover Publications.

Perlmutter, H. V. 1969. The tortuous evolution of the multinational corporation. *Columbia Journal of World Business*, 4(1): 9–18.

Pettigrew, A. 1992. On studying managerial elites. *Strategic Management Journal*, 13 (Winter): 163–182.

Podsakoff, P. M., & Organ, D. W. 1986. Self-reports in organizational research: problems and prospects. *Journal of Management*, 12(4): 531–544.

Porter, M. 1980. *Competitive Strategy*. New York: Free Press.

Porter, M. E. (ed.) 1986. *Competition in global industries*. Boston: Harvard Business School Press.

Prahalad, C., & Hamel, G. 1991. The core competence of the corporation. *Harvard Business Review*, 68(3): 79–91.

Prahalad, C. K., & Doz, Y. L. 1987. *The multinational mission*. New York: The Free Press.

Radner, R. 1975. A behavioral model of cost reduction. *Bell Journal of Economics and Management Science*, 6: 196–215.

Reger, R. K., & Palmer, T. B. 1996. Managerial categorizations of competitors: Using old maps to navigate new environments. *Organization Science*, 7(1): 22–39.

Reuber, A. R., & Fisher, E. 1997. The influence of the management team's international experience on the internationalization behaviors of SMEs. *Journal of International Business Studies*, 28(4): 807–825.

Rhinesmith, S. H. 1993. *A manager's guide to globalization: Six keys to success in a changing world*. Homewood: Irwin.

Ross, L., & Nisbett, R. E. 1991. *The person and the situation: Perspectives of social psychology*. New York: McGraw-Hill.

Roth, K. 1995. Managing international interdependence: CEO characteristics in a resource-based framework. *Academy of Management Journal*, 38(1): 200–231.

Sambharya, R. 1996. Foreign experience of top management teams and international diversification strategies of U.S. multinational corporations. *Strategic Management Journal*, 17(9): 739–746.

Sanders, W. G., & Carpenter, M. A. 1998. Internationalization and firm governance: The roles of CEO compensation, top team composition, and board structure. *Academy of Management Journal*, 41: 158–178.

Scott, W. R. 1995. *Institutions and organizations*. Thousands Oaks, CA: Sage.

Selznick, P. 1957. *Leadership in administration: A sociological interpretation*. Evanston, IL: Row and Peterson.

Shiffrin, R. M. 1988. Attention. In S. S. Stevens, & R. C. Atkinson (eds), *Steven's handbook of experimental psychology*. New York: Wiley.

Shiffrin, R. M., & Schneider, W. 1977. Controlled and automatic human information processing: II. Perceptual learning, automatic attending, and a general theory. *Psychological Review*, 84(2): 127–190.

Shortell, S. M., & Zajac, E. J. 1990. Perceptual and archival measures of Miles and Snow's strategic types: A comprehensive assessment of reliability and validity. *Academy of Management Journal*, 33(4): 817–832.

Simon, H. A. 1982. Designing organizations for an information rich world. In H. A. Simon (ed.), *Models of bounded rationality: Behavioral economics and business organization*, Vol. 2: 171–185. Cambridge, MA: The MIT Press.

Simon, H. A. 1997. *Administrative behavior: A study of decision making processes in administrative organizations* (4th ed.). New York: The Free Press.

Sokolov, E. i. N. 1963. *Perception and the conditioned reflex*. Oxford: Pergamon Press.

Sproull, L. S. 1984. The nature of managerial attention. In L. S. Sproull, & P. D. Larkey (eds), *Advances in information processing in organizations*, Vol. 1: 9–27. Greenwich, CT: JAI Press.

Stinchcombe, A. L. 1968. *Constructing social theories*. Chicago: Chicago University Press.

Swidler, A. 1986. Culture in action: Symbols and strategies. *American Sociological Review*, 51: 273–286.

Szulanski, G. 1996. Exploring internal stickiness: Impediments to the transfer of best practice within the firm. *Strategic Management Journal*, 17 (Winter Special Issue): 27–43.

Teece, D. J., Pisano, G., & Shuen, A. 1997. Dynamic capabilities and strategic management. *Strategic Management Journal*, 18(7): 509–533.

Titchener, E. B. 1908. *Lectures on the elementary psychology of feeling and attention*. New York: The Macmillan Company.

Toffler, A., & Toffler, H. 1993. *War and anti-war: Survival at the dawn of the 21st century* (1st ed.). Boston: Little Brown.

Treisman, A. M. 1969. Strategies and models of selective attention. *Psychological Review*, 76(3): 282–299.

Uleman, J. S. 1989. A framework for thinking intentionally about unintended thoughts. In J. S. Uleman, & J. A. Bargh (eds), *Unintended thoughts*: 425–449. New York: The Guilford Press.

Van de Ven, A. H. 1979. Review of Howard E. Aldrich's Organizations and Environments. *Administrative Science Quarterly*, 24: 320–325.

Vernon, R. 1966. International investment and international trade in the product cycle. *Quarterly Journal of Economics*, 80(2): 190–207.

Walsh, J. P. 1995. Managerial and organizational cognition: notes from a trip down memory lane. *Organization Science*, 6(3): 280–321.

Watson, J. B. 1914. *Behavior: An introduction to comparative psychology*. New York: Henry Holt and company.

Weick, K. 1993. Collective mind in organizations: Heedful interrelating on flights decks. *Administrative Science Quarterly*, 38(3): 357–381.

Weick, K. E. 1979. *The social psychology of organizing* (2nd ed.). New York, NY: McGraw-Hill.

Weick, K. E., & Van Orden, P. W. 1990. Organizing on a global scale: a research and teaching agenda. *Human Resource Management*, 29(1): 49–61.

Wernerfelt, B. 1984. A resource-based view of the firm. *Strategic Management Journal*, 5(2): 171–180.

White, J. D., & Carlston, D. E. 1983. Consequences of schemata for attention, impressions and recall in complex social interactions. *Journal of Personality and Social Psychology*, 45(3): 538–549.

White, R. E., & Poynter, T. A. 1990. Organizing for worldwide advantage. In C. A. Bartlett, Y. L. Doz, & G. Hedlund (eds), *Managing the global firm*: 95–113. New York: Routledge.

Wickens, C. A. 1984. Processing resources in attention. In R. Parasuraman, & D. R. Davies (eds), *Varieties of attention*: 63–102. New York: Academic Press.

Winter, S. G. 1987. Knowledge and competence as strategic assets. In D. J. Teece (ed.), *The competitive challenge: Strategies for industrial innovation and renewal*, Vol. XI: 159–184. Cambridge, MA: Ballinger.

Wundt, W. M., & Judd, C. H. 1897. *Outlines of psychology*. Leipzig, New York: W. Engelmann and G. E. Stechert.

Yin, R. K. 1989. *Case Study Research*. Newbury Park, California: Sage Publications, Inc.

Zaheer, S. 1995. Overcoming the liability of foreignness. *Academy of Management Journal*, 38(2): 341–363.

Zander, U., & Kogut, B. 1995. Knowledge and the speed of the transfer and imitation of organizational capabilities: An empirical test. *Organization Science*, 6: 76–92.

Index